Rebel Beauty for Teens

7 Ways to Unleash Your unique Brand of Gorgeousness

by bethan christopher

 TRIGGER™

The mental health & wellbeing publisher

DEDICATED TO MY DAUGHTER, AYSHA-JADE

First published in 2021
This edition published in 2023 by Trigger Publishing
An imprint of Shaw Callaghan Ltd

UK Office
The Stanley Building
7 Pancras Square
Kings Cross
London N1C 4AG

US Office
On Point Executive Center, Inc
3030 N Rocky Point Drive W
Suite 150
Tampa, FL 33607

www.triggerhub.org

A CIP catalogue record for this book is available upon request from the British Library

ISBN: 978-1-83796-366-9

Project editor: Daniel Hurst
Cover design: John Tulip
Designer: Georgie Hewitt

CONTENTS

A Note from Trigger's Consultant Clinical Psychologist and Co-Founder, Lauren Callaghan

"Body confidence is key to good self-esteem. This wonderful interactive guided journal for teenagers to work through helps them to explore what body image is and how it is connected to their self-esteem and beliefs of self-worth. *REBEL BEAUTY FOR TEENS* will actively encourage and help any teenager to improve their self-confidence by having a healthy and positive relationship with their body, inside and out. As a psychologist, and a mother with daughters, I am delighted a book like this exists for young women."

I BELONG TO YOU! Draw, colour, write, doodle, scribble, cut, stick and unleash your creativity all over these pages to make this book as wonderfully unique as you are!

Introduction

She nibbles on strawberries whilst sunning her legs on a pool-side lounger. You munch on a bag of crisps and gulp back a drink before dashing for the bus. She laughs and presses a perfectly manicured finger to her cheek as she slinks down to the shoreline. You hug your towel tightly to your chest, chatter nervously with your friends and leg it to the sea. She's been goading you for not being skinnier and more attractive ever since you were a little girl and thought that being a princess was a career choice.

Who is she? Meet Ideal Beauty.

 Ideal Beauty is the embodiment of the shape, look, weight and appearance that **is supposed** to make up **the perfect babe** (according to the media, ad agencies and people who make billions of dollars from diet pills). Ideal Beauty sprawls across magazine covers and flashes her icy white smile from every angle of your news feed. Her image is used to sell everything from cars and clothes to holidays and smoothies. Her face is the filter that your friends apply to their selfies before they post a pic on social media, and you just need to look to her to find the latest trends for eyebrow shaping, neck contouring, leg buffing and knee powdering.

Ideal Beauty is not real. She is photoshopped, airbrushed, filtered and edited. But despite being unattainable, she taps on your shoulder hundreds of times a day whispering, "Be like me. Strive for me. If you're like me, you will be happy."

Ideal Beauty isn't one person. She is the collective face of the non-stop barrage of unattainable beauty that bombards girls, and increasingly boys, on a daily basis. These photos of shiny-toothed, smiling, slim, toned, flawless, picture-perfect goddesses hurl themselves at us like self-esteem attacking ninjas from the instant we wake to the moment we go to sleep. The crazy thing is that we're so used to it that many of us don't even notice it's happening.

Instead, we think this:

- "I need to get thinner."

- "I need to be louder."

- "I need to get my style sorted."

- "If I get attention from the popular kids, I'll be happy."

- "I need to wear more make-up."

- "I need more followers/likes."

"I need abs."

 "I should look more like Belinda Babe-alicious/Mylie Stylie/ Kim Karglamorous."

What pretty much NO ONE realises is that Ideal Beauty has been designed to **deliberately rob** us of the feelings of beauty we were born with. From a very young age, we have been systematically immersed in messages that tell us we need to be prettier, thinner, blonder, straighter, curvier or just different to how we look right now.

The result? Our girl-gang's collective body-love is under major attack, with studies showing that when girls and women have hang-ups about their looks, they often fail to reach their full potential in life. Girls have been reported to skip school, duck out of sports, cancel social events and even avoid putting their hand up in class to speak out because they're scared of being judged on how they look. Our sisters from other misters are missing out on taking part in parties, panels and performances, choosing instead to shrink back and try to make themselves small and invisible, too scared to show up and be heard... all because they don't feel attractive enough.

Does this sound wrong to you?

Do you believe that something should be done to change this?

Are you up for being one of the warriors who help trigger this change?

Are you tired of feeling bad about yourself and ready to feel beautiful in your own skin?

If you've answered yes to any of these questions, then you're in the right place.

Never before in history have women and girls been more free, more able and more capable of changing the world or how they participate within it. This book gives you the chance to be part of a revolution - something that could unleash women's power into the world in a way that it's never been unleashed before. It's going to give you a chance to design and test out a whole new version of beauty that's not bottled, branded or sold on the shelves of your local store. No one will tell us about this version of beauty - because there's only one person who can access it: **YOU**.

This version of beauty is off the beaten track, veering away from the crowds and is for people who believe in individuality and making up their own rules about what is good enough. It is fueled by how we feel about ourselves on the inside, how **WE** choose to look at the world and the gorgeousness **WE** can experience when we embrace who **WE** truly are.

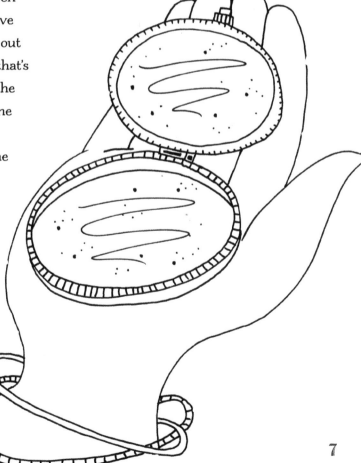

Who am I?

My name is Bethan. For over 20 years, I have been on a wild, twisty mission to work out what Ideal Beauty is all about and how we ladies can disentangle ourselves from her. I've tracked down history's greatest beauty bluffers (who, by no coincidence, were also the beauty industry's first millionaires), to find out how Ideal Beauty has ended up with so much power and influence. I've dug down deep into Ideal Beauty's past, stalked her social media and lifted the curtain on who really pulls her strings.

Here are some things that I discovered along the way.

THING 1: Ideal Beauty is just an idea.

She's a thrown together hotch-potch of ideas that have been developed by the cosmetic and advertising industries. This toxic concoction has been mixed up with technology, sprinkled with some cultural shifty bits (what is going in society at any one time) and, ta-dah!, we have one fully formed idea of what it means to be beautiful.

The trouble with ideas is that when we grow up surrounded by them – and everyone we know believes them – we tend to buy into them without question. Then, in no time at all, we're comparing ourselves negatively to what we think we should look like. Most people will find they don't measure up to Ideal Beauty's crazy standards (even the model who posed for the image doesn't match the picture). This mismatch creates an internal dilemma that impacts on our self-image, mood and behaviour. The good news is that, with a little bit of unpicking, we can deconstruct the ideas we have of Ideal Beauty and get her acrylic nails **out** of our minds, bodies and bank accounts.

Exercise: Cram the box below with any thoughts you have about beauty. You can write anything, from the diet your sister is on, to something your friend's dad once said about a pretty woman on TV, to whether YOU think beauty is a positive or negative thing. If you need more space, grab a spare piece of paper and keep going on that – stick or staple any extra notes to this page once you're done to keep all your thoughts in one place.

THING 2: Ideal Beauty has a bazillion different looks.

In the UK, women pluck and shape their eyebrows, sometimes removing them completely and then tattooing the shape back on, whereas in Uzbekistan women are encouraged to cultivate their monobrows. In America, women spend hundreds of dollars to reduce puffiness around their eyes, whilst women in Korea are doing everything they can to achieve fuller eyebags. Known as **aegyo sal**, which means "eye smiles", Korean women use make-up, sticky plastic, commercial fillers and fat grafts to give their eyelids that heavy-bottomed look.

Wherever you are in the world and at whichever point in history you happen to have your nose in this book, there will always be a certain set of looks – and ways of behaving – that the beauty police are telling you to conform to. Your family, friends, community and personal experiences will also add to your unique perspective on what Ideal Beauty should be. In the past, the pressure to look perfect weighed heaviest on women, but now the need to have a perfect body is pressing down on the guys too. Bottom line? We're all in this together.

Exercise: Use the box below to write down how you think a person's body should be in order to look good. Here are a few words to prompt you: hair, nails, skin, nose, eyebrows, eyes, lips, neck, jaw, breasts, shape, legs, stomach, nails, hands, arms, shoulders, genitals, feet, toes.

THING 3: Ideal Beauty is a shape-shifting illusion.

Yup. This sounds kind of creepy. Allow me to explain.

On the 25th August, 1939, a film called **The Wizard of Oz** was released. At the end of the movie, Dorothy's dog, Toto, pulls down a huge curtain to reveal that the great and powerful wizard Oz is in fact just a massive light projection on a wall – an illusion. Prior to this, Dorothy spends the whole story believing that Oz the wizard is going to help her, but when the curtain comes down she realises that Oz is simply an illusion that is being controlled by a funny little man with a green suit. This is also how it works with Ideal Beauty.

The fashion, cosmetic and diet industries project this great and powerful airbrushed image of Ideal Beauty up on to all our screens and devices, wooing us with an illusion of perfection and convincing us that we are looking at something real and achievable. We then spend our precious money and time buying products to achieve this perfect look. Yet, just as we think we've managed to achieve the perfect eyebrows or pencil-thin wrists,

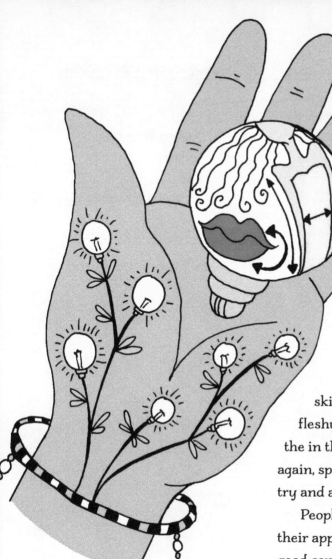

skinny earlobes when NOW fleshy, juicy, dangly earlobes are the in thing. We then set off, once again, spending time and money to try and attain the new look.

People who are unhappy with their appearance are exceptionally good consumers. As a result, the global beauty industry is worth around £400 billion, and while the illusion of Ideal Beauty helps the diet and cosmetic industries continue to get richer, it comes at a great cost to the mental and physical wellbeing of girls and women all over the world.

WHAM!, the image of Ideal Beauty shape-shifts into something else.

Ideal Beauty's new look then smiles down at us and we're left wondering why we have spent our entire existence trying to attain

Exercise: Write down in the box below everything you know of that women do/buy in order to achieve Ideal Beauty. For example, cosmetic procedures, make-up, strange diets and so on.

_____

_____

_____

_____

_____

_____

_____

_____

_____

_____

_____

THING 4: There's another version of beauty that no one told us about.

Right now some people might be thinking, "Whoa, hang on a minute. If Ideal Beauty is a sham, money-making ploy, who is going to tell me how I should look and what will I do with my time? I need Ideal Beauty in my life!"

And this, in all seriousness, is a valid point. We are so used to being told what to do by our mums, dads, teachers, friends, aunts, uncles, TV shows, phones and social media feeds that taking back our power and sense of self can be daunting. And overwhelming. And confusing.

We spend disproportionate amounts of time thinking and focusing our energy on searching for Ideal Beauty, which might involve comparing ourselves with other girls, watching online beauty tutorials, obsessing about what size we are or stalking pretty people's social media accounts. The thought of letting go of one of our major pastimes is really scary.

STOP! Don't panic. Take a deep breath.

By the final page of this book, you will have a step-by-step process that allows you to access the gorgeousness tucked away inside of you. You'll be able to amplify it and switch it up whenever you want to. You'll feel beautiful. Simply by being you. All you need to do is complete the exercises in this book, stay the course and be prepared to experience your version of Rebel Beauty.

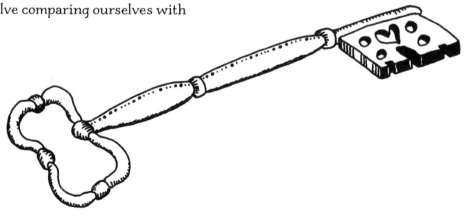

Exercise: Fill in the permission slip below, allowing yourself permission to explore your own version of beauty, take part in this process, stay the course and learn to unleash your own unique gorgeousness.

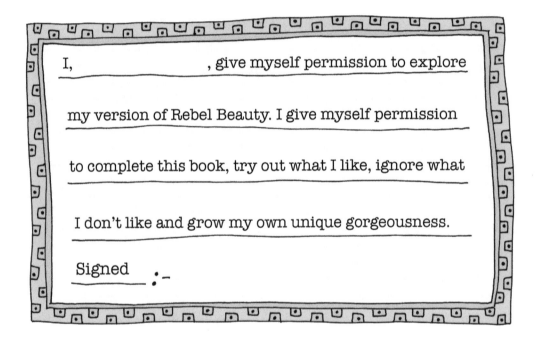

I, _____, give myself permission to explore

my version of Rebel Beauty. I give myself permission

to complete this book, try out what I like, ignore what

I don't like and grow my own unique gorgeousness.

Signed _____ :-

What happens now?

The book you are holding contains everything you need to know and do to access your own version of beautiful. It's packed with battle-proven activities, nuggets of creative genius and bits of tried-and-tested mayhem that will help you to unleash your gorgeousness.

Rebel Beauty for Teens is divided into seven parts, which you can work through one by one and then return to at any point. The final chapter, **Rebel Practice** (p.156-175), will show you how to bring everything you've learned together and integrate your version of Rebel Beauty into everyday life.

The most important thing to remember is that this isn't school. In fact, it's the opposite of school. It's messy, timetable-free and there's no routine or plan to any of it. You can try out whatever you like, throw it around and, if it doesn't stick, ditch it. Who cares?

Like Rebel Beauty, this book is anti-perfection. You can make the contents as messy as you like, fold down pages, rip sheets out and scrawl all over it with a biro if required. If you're on a roll and need more space to write, stick in extra pages. You can even use this book to rest your head on if you don't have a pillow. It's going to be your companion for a while now. And it will still love you even if you throw it out of a window.

This book has got your back.

And it's about to take you backpacking out of the world of Ideal Beauty and way off the known track, into the big, bold, brilliant landscape of Rebel Beauty.

Are you ready? Let's go!

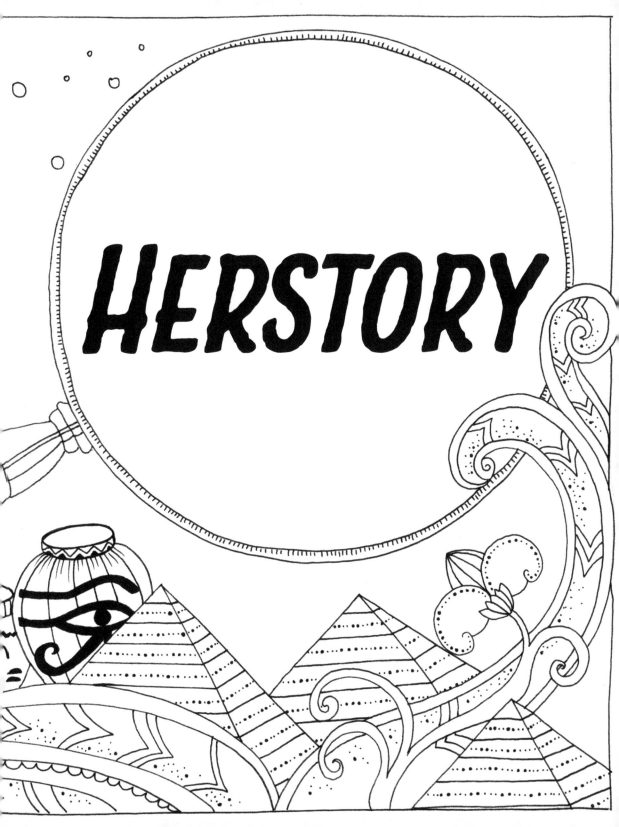

Ideal Beauty: The Backstory

Just like a love-to-hate character in your favourite box-set, Ideal Beauty has a twisty-turny, scandal-filled backstory. Originally, I planned to give you that backstory in all of its gory detail. You were going to get all the ins and outs on how wanting to look - and feel - attractive is an innate human desire that's been with us since the dawn of time, when we were still sleeping in caves and fashioning crop tops from palm leaves and the tails of unsuspecting beavers.

I **WAS** going to throw in some bits and bobs on:

♥ How Ancient Egyptian "it-girls" used kohl, a black paste made from ground up minerals, as eyeliner to mimic the elongated eyes of their gods and goddesses, who for them represented the highest standards of beauty.

♥ How Renaissance noblewomen in Europe used dangerous potions, made by boiling snakeskins in wine, because they believed they made their complexions bright, in their quest for Ideal Beauty.

♥ How Medieval European women plucked their hairlines so that they would look more like the innocent, large-foreheaded virginal maidens of early Christianity.

I **WAS** totally going to weave in some cool subplots, such as:

♥ How, in 1903, a young Polish woman called Helena Rubinstein emigrated to Australia and quickly recognised that the harsh climate, hot sun and strong winds meant that people's skin took a severe weather-beating. Recognising that many women were seeking to remedy this, Helena opened a one-room beauty salon and invented a face cream that she then sold with the promise that it would make her customers' complexions clear and flawless. Scientifically, the cream did nothing but that didn't stop the homemade skin-care product from selling out. By 1915, Helena was the world's first self-made female millionaire – and arguably the brain that birthed the beauty industry as we know it today.

How, in around 1860, photography and the use of cameras became a mainstream pursuit and, for the first time ever, people were able to obtain a visual image of themselves and witness how other people saw them. Early photographers, who made a living taking portraits of wealthy Victorians, soon started to use special lenses to soften pictures and blur the skin, hiding the pores and pockmarks of their hard-to-please clients. It was these soft-focus-style photographic images, devoid of blemishes and wrinkles, that Helena Rubinstein and other beauty companies later used to advertise their products, suggesting that the smooth appearance of the skin was down to their creams, as opposed to some serious filters. Female consumers no longer admired the attractive women in their own communities and instead began to aspire to the faces they saw in these adverts. The heights of Ideal Beauty had just moved even further out of reach.

How, in 1987, the photo-editing tool, Photoshop was born and, almost immediately, it and Ideal Beauty formed a dynamic duo. With Ideal Beauty's unrealistic standards and Photoshop's editing abilities, together they were able to remove offending inches from model's waists, puff up dresses, jut-out collarbones, minimise crooked noses, tighten skin, enlarge breasts and eradicate anything deemed mildly flawed from a model's body with the click of a button. Suddenly, the pictures that were shoved into the faces of women and girls in adverts and magazines were no longer those of real women. And, with Ideal Beauty now delivering a digitally enhanced visage for the public to aspire to, the magicians of the flesh - cosmetic surgeons - stepped in to offer women Botox, face-lifts, implants, jaw reshaping, plumping, lifting and various other procedures so they could try and keep up with the new ever-shifting beauty ideals.

But then ... I thought, **NO**. Enough of the backstory.

Ideal Beauty has had way too much airtime already! We know she's tied us ladies in knots, stuffed us into corsets, caked our face in foundation and threatened to label us as ugly if we don't abide by her rules. We know that through the Barbie dolls we played with as kids, the narrow representation of women in pop-music videos, the perfect actresses in Hollywood movies and the celebrities we've seen on TV.

We already know that these ideas about beauty have preoccupied our time and stolen our energy. So, do we really need to hear any more about Ideal Beauty? NOPE.

Is it time to move forward from this point onwards? **Yes. Definitely.**

And this starts with **YOU**.

Rebel Beauty: The Rewrite

Rebel Beauty for Teens: Seven Ways to Unleash Your Unique Brand of Gorgeousness is not about Ideal Beauty.

It's about **YOU**.

This book is going to give you everything you need to bring your personal version of Rebel Beauty onto the centre stage of your life. The spotlight is going to be on exploring your unique brand of gorgeousness, what makes you special and how you can boldly, confidently express yourself in the world going forward.

The ideas and exercises within these pages come from a combination of places. Some have emerged from my years of coaching work, both with adults and people of your age. Some of them have come from my own mentors and role models, both men and women. Other parts have come from my own personal journey, through hitting beauty-rock-bottom and finding the tools and resources to recognise my own unique brand of beauty and reclaim my sense of self-worth.

People often ask me whether Rebel Beauty is inner beauty. My response to this is that when we start to change the way we see ourselves on the inside and stop needing validation around how we look on the outside, this shift radiates outwards in the way we look, act, speak and behave. By fully embodying our beauty on the inside, it's as though something in us is lit up. I call this "The Cleopatra Effect".

The Cleopatra Effect

Ever heard of Cleopatra? Born in Egypt, though of Greek blood, in her time Cleopatra was known as the world's most beautiful (and powerful!) woman. Throughout history, this diva has inspired thousands of works of art, countless films and is still known as a pearl-dissolving, milk-bathing Queen badass. On the surface, Cleopatra may seem one of the earliest Ideal Beauty icons and yet the writings of the Greek historian, Plutarch, suggest that Cleopatra didn't actually fit the cookie-cutter mould of Ideal Beauty at that time.

Plutarch said, "For her beauty, as we are told, was in itself not altogether incomparable, nor such as to strike those who saw her; but to converse with her had an irresistible charm and her presence... had something stimulating about it."

Plutarch nods towards Cleopatra blending a combo of self-awareness, body confidence and rock-solid trust in her own capabilities into a unique form of gorgeousness that was enough to make people want to be near to her. By activating her beauty on the inside, she displayed something on the outside that was compelling and undeniably powerful.

By working through the seven elements of Rebel Beauty explored in this book, you too are going to unlock and bring forth your own unique gorgeousness.

The seven elements that you are going to unlock are:

Rebel Eyes. Where you choose to focus your attention determines what you experience. When you reclaim your brain back from what the media tells you is beautiful, you can start to define yourself and your beauty, on your own terms.

Rebel Body. Ideal Beauty promotes the idea that when you have the perfect outer body, you will finally feel good inside, too. By reversing this idea and redesigning how you label yourself, you can build a rock-solid relationship with the one thing that will be with you for the rest of your life: your body.

Rebel Voice. Communication is one of your sharpest tools for expressing your gorgeousness. This isn't about whether you are chatty or quiet. It's about how to walk your talk and verbalise your needs with courage, confidence and clarity.

Rebel Passion: You know when you're in the zone. Things flow, anxiety lessens and you feel at ease and in control. Your passions are what help you enter that zone. They point towards your unique talents and how you can make your life, and this world, a better place.

Rebel Power: For centuries the female menstrual cycle has been a subject of shame and secrecy. Yet within this monthly cycle lies one of our biggest superpowers as women. Crack the code, crown your cycle and communicate with your body in a whole new way.

Rebel Purpose: You're here for a reason. You're reading this book for a reason.

By reclaiming your whole self and redefining your ideas about your body and your beauty, you're in the perfect position to find your true purpose and live a legendary life.

Rebel Practice: Having used the tools in this book to discover your Rebel Beauty, the final stage is to bring those practices into your life and make them habits. It's through daily discipline that change happens and your gorgeousness can be unleashed on the world.

There. The backstory is told. Rebel Beauty is in the building.

Now, let's get this SHOW on the road.

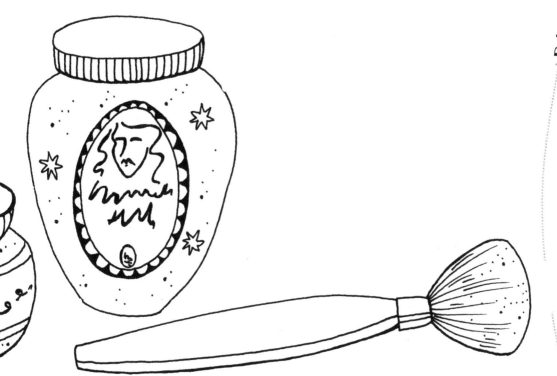

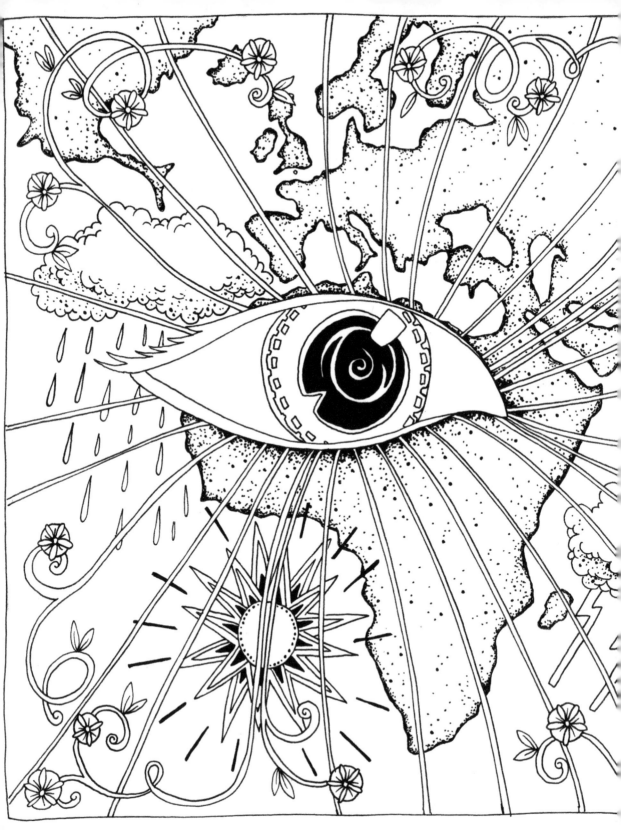

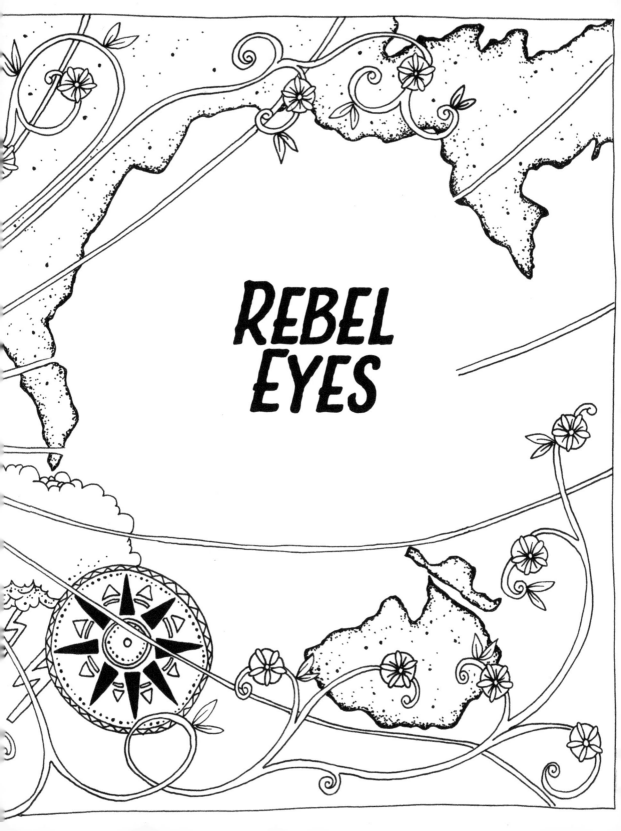

Seeing Things Differently

Two sisters, Jade and Ruby, take a trip to the big city. Jade is in her element. She loves the cacophony of noise, the vibrant colours and the melting pot of different cultures and cuisines. She's excited to visit the cool shops, gaze up at the massive buildings and immerse herself in the pulsing life of the city. She visits famous art galleries, posts a selfie from a famous bridge and calls her mum from a historical monument, saying "this place is awesome! I want to live here!" She loves the sense of busy-ness and yeah, it's expensive, but that just motivates her to study hard and get good grades so that she can get a great job and live and work here when she's older.

Ruby, meanwhile, isn't feeling it. She hates crowds and she can't stand it when people jostle her when they walk by, especially since her friend told her about all the pickpockets and muggings that happen in big towns. Trailing her sister through busy streets, Ruby's nose wrinkles at the smell of the pollution in the air. The gutters are overflowing with rubbish, shady characters loiter in doorways and her senses are assaulted by the noise of people shouting, music blaring, horns sounding impatiently and the smoggy exhalations of rumbling engines, all of which makes her head spin. Visiting the art galleries and sightseeing is okay, but to be honest, Ruby can't wait to get out of there – and she's not planning on coming back any time soon.

This is the same city – the same trip – but the two sisters see things very differently. Their expectations and preconceptions colour their experience, so where Jade sees vitality and opportunity, Ruby sees danger and pollution.

The Shades of Perception

We don't just see with our eyes. Everything you experience in life is filtered through your own perception... the way **YOU** choose to see something.

A little like wearing an invisible pair of sunglasses, your mood, energy and beliefs all combine to give you a unique "tinted" view of the world. These "shades of perception" determine what you see, how you act, how you think, what you say and what you do in different situations. Ultimately, our "shades of perception" can either make the world look wonderful, terrifying or anything in between. We then act, according to what we "see".

Think about the days when you just can't shake the fug

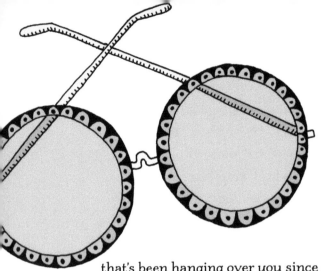

that's been hanging over you since breakfast. Maybe you wake up, look around your room and think "urgh, it's so ugly – I could never bring friends here." Perhaps you glance in the mirror and all you can see is the massive pimple on your lip. Maybe your little brother tries to make you laugh at breakfast, but only succeeds in irritating you. You slam the door as you leave the house and the more the grump sets in, the more everything – and everyone - gets on your nerves.

When you're feeling moody, your mind will seek and find anything that backs up your belief that your life sucks. It hears the thought "I hate my life" and then gears up to deliver every last shred of evidence to support that idea.

The more your brain picks out that evidence, the grumpier you become and so the cycle goes on.

Alternatively, imagine you've just had some brilliant news. Your favourite band is in town and your mum has bought you and your best friends tickets as a surprise! You go to school and it doesn't matter that you're faced with double algebra (or whatever your least-favourite lesson is) first thing, because your sunny mood wins through and all you can focus on is how great your life is. At breaktime you ooze positivity and fun and people seem to swarm around you and enjoy your company more as a result. You feel confident. Yay! Life is good. Why though? Because your "shades of perception" are like filters that colour your view of the world, and when your mind is looking for the good stuff in life, that's what it will generally find.

If you're still not convinced about how your perception colours your world, try this:

REBEL EYES EXERCISE 1: Seeing Red

Stop what you're doing and put this book down in front of you. Now look around the room that you're in. Give yourself 30 seconds to count every red object you can see. Do not read on until you've counted all of the red.

Okay, done? Now, on the line below note down how many **green** things you saw – not red, but green.

Impossible to do because you only counted the red things in the room? That's because you were actively **looking** for the red things. You gave your mind an instruction and it did what it was told. Likewise, your mind will always find what you look for in your life whether positive, negative or something in between.

Think back to Jade and Ruby (p.30). Jade went looking for all the good stuff in the city and she saw it. Ruby looked for the bad and she saw that. In this way, our "shades of perception" colour our view of the world. In fact, they colour how we see everything: our homes, families, friends... even **ourselves!**

Rose-Tinted Glasses

The way you see yourself – and what you habitually look for in yourself – is known as self-esteem.

Your self-esteem is your ultimate pair of invisible shades. It defines what **YOU** see when **YOU** look in the mirror. It defines what you believe people think about you. If ten people paid you a compliment, but just one person made a snarky criticism, your self-esteem is what determines who you listen to. It is what steers you towards relationships that make you and helps you avoid the ones that will break you. Or, too often, the other way around.

Individuals who see themselves through a lens of low self-esteem often perceive others as being more attractive, intelligent or successful than themselves. This can make social situations agonising and relationships a challenge. When someone experiencing low self-esteem makes a mistake, their shades of perception will magnify that mistake to seem WAAAAY bigger than it is. The person then becomes hypersensitive to criticism which can mean that decision-making is almost impossible for fear of making the wrong choice. Another behaviour associated with low self-esteem is the excessive need to please others. This may lead someone to feeling pressurised into doing things that they

REBEL EYES EXERCISE 2: Mirror Mirror

Finish the sentences below with brutal honesty.

My personality is ....

My fashion sense is ....

I'm good at ....

I'm bad at ....

My life is ....

My body is ....

I see myself as being ....

Look back at your answers. Would you say that your self-esteem is high, medium or low? Are some sentences positive? Are there areas of your self-perception that could do with some serious revamping?

Whatever shades of self-esteem you're currently looking through, try not to judge yourself. Nothing that you have written is a concrete fact. Each sentence is simply a perception that your mind has collected evidence to support. It doesn't reflect how anyone else sees you **AT ALL**. The good news is, just like a cheap pair of sunglasses, these perceptions can be changed.

later regret, for example sending nudes online, using drugs and alcohol or shoplifting.

Those who see themselves through the lens of high self-esteem have a very different experience of themselves and the world. Their view of life tends to be coloured by a strong set of values and principles that guides them. They make choices based upon these principles, can trust their own judgement and don't feel guilty if others don't agree. They feel capable of solving problems, ask for help if needed and see themselves as equal to others, regardless of differences in ability, wealth, body shape or social media following.

How do you see yourself? When you think about yourself, do you focus on your good bits, limitations or a mixture of both? Do you believe that you are as good as other people?

Upgrading Your Shades

The key to upgrading your self-esteem is to look for the gorgeousness

inside you and to repeat this process every day. Forever. Sound hard? It's really not – once you realise how brilliant you are, you'll be the number-one member of your own fan club for life! The hard bit is appreciating your own brilliance in

"WE DON'T SEE
THE WORLD AS IT IS.
WE SEE THE WORLD
AS WE ARE."

Anaïs Nin

the first place. Right now, we live in a world that does everything it can to encourage low self-esteem. The media tells us that if we have **this body, this hair, this house, this item of clothing** then we'll be happy – and that, by definition, we can't be happy just as we are. A heady mix of Hollywood, Netflix and social media tricks us into thinking that our happiness, our very success as human beings, can be equated to the house we live in, the money we have in the bank and the face that reflects back at us when we look in the mirror. Even the schools we attend grade our "good-enough-ness" on how well we can **do this algebra, write this essay** and perform in **this national under-16s athletics competition.**

Because most of what we're told about our worth seems to be based on an outer source, it's really easy to compare ourselves to others.

We compare our bodies to the Insta models. We compare our homes to the rich kids on TV. We compare our parents, our families, our wardrobes, our grades, and with every comparison we are asking ourselves the questions, "Am I good enough? Do I measure up?" We start to actively focus on the parts of ourselves that don't quite fit these supposed ideals... and guess what? That's right, our mind then FINDS the evidence to support our focus.

As a species, we have been brainwashed into looking for the limitation and lack in ourselves and our lives. To turn this around requires a form of counter self-brainwashing. In other words, we have to get into a habit of looking for – and focusing on – other things. What you focus on defines your experience, so it's up to you to start defining yourself.

Try Some Rebel Eyes For Size

On the following pages you will find a set of activities to help you upgrade your "shades of perception". These Rebel Beauty shades will help to retrain your eyes to find the REAL beauty in the world, your environment and yourself. The more you get into the habit of seeing this way, the more natural it will become.

Seeing Things Differently

REBEL EYES EXERCISE 3: Open Your Eyes

Look out of the nearest window and find something beautiful. Not the things that we're told are beautiful (i.e. the person who looks like they've stepped straight off the air-brushed cover of a fashion magazine). Look for real beauty – **Rebel Beauty**. This could be a bird flying through the sky, the natural patterns in the wood on a fence, an elderly couple holding hands as they walk down the road. Don't move from the window until you've found ten things that are truly beautiful in the world outside. If you aren't near a window, make a list of beautiful things in your surrounding area. **Once you've made your list, draw all of the beauty you see in the space opposite.**

1 ....

2 ....

3 ....

4 ....

5 ....

6 ....

7 ....

8 ....

9 ....

10 ....

Seeing Things Differently

REBEL EYES EXERCISE 4: Take a Long, Hard Look at Yourself

Use the space below to write down everything that is beautiful about YOU. Think about things you've done, said and tried to help with. Think about the beautiful ideas you've had, friendships you've been part of, things you've created and people you've made smile. Write down any beautiful dreams you've had, places you've been and memories you've made. Don't move until you've written ten beautiful things about yourself.

1 ....

2 ....

3 ....

4 ....

5 ....

6 ....

7 ....

8 ....

9 ....

10 ....

REBEL EYES EXERCISE 5: Look Up

A role model is someone who you aspire to be like, look up to and admire. This person may be any gender or age. They may be on TV, live in your neighbourhood, be a family member, a teacher or a friend. They may be a character in a film or book, or even be someone you've learnt about in history class. Write down the names of three people you see as role models and then list some of the characteristics and the values they embody that you admire.

NAME:
....
....

What I admire about them:
....
....
....
....

NAME:
....
....

What I admire about them:
....
....
....
....

NAME:
....
....

What I admire about them:
....
....
....
....

It is said that when we see a quality we admire (or indeed dislike) in another person, it's because it's something that we have within us. For example, if the role model you wrote about in the last exercise is a woman who against all odds has changed the world and what you love about her is her passion and determination, that highlights the fact that **YOU** also have passion and determination inside you. We project our good stuff (and our bad, though that's another story) onto others, but the key is to recognise it and begin nurturing this in ourselves. Imagine that all the role model qualities that you wrote down on the previous page exist in you and all you need to do to let them out is to begin nurturing them.

Each day start looking for those qualities in yourself and bringing them forward whenever you can. Remember, **YOUR** perception is what brings you evidence, so if you are looking for the gorgeousness in you, your mind will have no choice but to show you all the clear evidence that you are as gorgeous as you believe.

DEFINE YOUR SELF.

"WITH EVERY EXPERIENCE
YOU ALONE ARE PAINTING
YOUR OWN CANVAS,
THOUGHT BY THOUGHT,
CHOICE BY CHOICE."

Oprah Winfrey

REBEL BODY

Your Body, Your Rules

Your body image is precious.

It is so precious that the weight-loss industry, the diet-sellers, the glossy magazines and the cosmetic surgeons will do anything to get their hands on it. It is so precious that billions of pounds are spent on advertising to try and snare it every year. Once captured – and battered around until it is bent all of out shape so that you don't recognise it any more – it will be passed back to you, distorted and overloaded with messages on how you should be thinner, curvier or prettier. It will now tell you that you are not good enough.

With all of these negative messages about how we need to fit in or shape up being internalised, people are putty in the hands of the beauty industry. Girls and women, boys and men are learning to hate how they look. They agonise over being too thin, too fat, too bony, too heavy, too broad, too flat-chested and then begin a life-long journey of trying (and inevitably failing) to find body acceptance through attempting multiple reshapes. But, here's the thing: whatever silhouette happens to be in vogue, your body is already a set shape.

This is the result of two things:

1 Your genetics. You might have your mum's eyes, your dad's jawline and the hands of your great auntie Maud who loved to wear purple hats and play the electric guitar. You are a physical cocktail of all your ancestry, mixed up and reformed into a unique combination of you-ness. Just like your family tree, your body is unique and something to be proud of, embraced and celebrated.

2 Once you've stopped growing, you body shape will also be affected by what you eat and how much exercise you get. Generally, if you eat a wholesome balanced diet and are physically active, your body should level into its own unique size and shape that will allow you to live your healthiest, most vital life. On the other hand, if you are in the habit of munching on processed foods and high-sugar snacks and glugging on energy drinks, and your main activity involves thumb scrolling on social media, your body will respond by getting sluggish and gaining some extra weight.

In the previous chapter, Rebel Eyes, you got all the juice on perception and self-esteem. You learnt that how you see yourself is a matter of opinion. In the same way, you may think your body looks awful, but someone else may see it as amazing. What really counts is recognising that your body is your greatest ally and treating it accordingly.

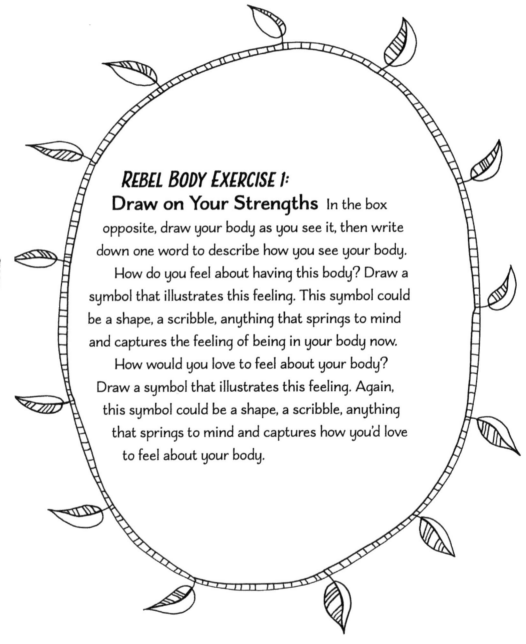

Rebel Body Exercise 1:
Draw on Your Strengths In the box opposite, draw your body as you see it, then write down one word to describe how you see your body.

How do you feel about having this body? Draw a symbol that illustrates this feeling. This symbol could be a shape, a scribble, anything that springs to mind and captures the feeling of being in your body now.

How would you love to feel about your body? Draw a symbol that illustrates this feeling. Again, this symbol could be a shape, a scribble, anything that springs to mind and captures how you'd love to feel about your body.

Draw a picture of how you see your body

DRAW A SYMBOL THAT REPRESENTS HOW YOU CURRENTLY FEEL ABOUT YOUR BODY

Draw a symbol that represents how you'd like to feel about your body

I see my body as: ....

....

Your Body, Your B.F.F

Whether you believe it right now or not, your body is an incredible vehicle that is here to transport you through your life with flair, gorgeousness and ease. You are born with it and you will die with it. You can make it your best friend or your worst enemy, who you will spend your whole life battling with.

We buy into the concept that by changing our outer body, we can change our inner experience of feeling good enough to ourselves and others, but actually the opposite is true. Choose to befriend your body, define it in positive ways and build a healthy relationship with it and you'll begin to value it, look after it and express yourself with it. This is when feelings of inner gorgeousness begin to grow.

Loving your body is an act of beauty rebellion. Here are three steps to get started in building a rock-solid relationship with your lifelong B.F.F.

 BODY LOVE. Ditch the diets and get to know your best buddy: hang out, eat food, go dancing.

 BODY LANGUAGE. Learn body language tricks to change your mood and feel amazing.

BODY LABELS. Bring in empowering words to describe your astoundingly gorgeous bod and use them when talking about yourself.

Body Love

Ditch the Diets

Whether you are a meat-eater, vegan, veggie, flexitarian, paleo or plant-based, fuelling your body with food is undeniably important. Your skeleton doubles in volume during your teen years, so to hit your true height and maximum brain genius, you need to make sure that you are fuelling your bod with the right stuff.

When people get hung up on squeezing themselves into ideal body shapes, they'll often restrict the food they eat to lose weight. Faddy diets that starve our bodies of vital nutrients appear to offer speedy weight-loss gains, but what they actually offer is a feeling of being flaky, grumpy and so hungry that sugary processed foods become irresistible and taste overwhelmingly good.

Before they know what's happened, the person on the diet has gobbled seven packets of jelly sweets and four chocolate oranges, then instantly feels horrible and guiltily resolves to start their diet all over again - on Monday. This is an unhealthy pattern to get into.

If you want to have a body and brain that perform at peak power, you'll need to fuel your body with the super juice it requires.

Grub geeks, the Food Standards Agency, say that you need:

♥ Five portions of fruit and veg each day (i.e. two bits of fruit and three portions of veg).

♥ A portion of grains at every meal (that's oats, rice, wholegrain bread – not chocolate brownies and white bagels).

♥ Protein such as meat, fish or eggs or – if you're veg or vegan – nuts, soya, eggs and legumes (beans and peas etc).

♥ Three portions of calcium each day. Calcium can be found in milk products, such as cheese and yoghurt or soya milk if you are dairy-free.

Eat this stuff, drop the sugar, bin the take-out menus and see how much your energy, mood and body-love begin to charge up.

REBEL BODY EXERCISE 2: Nourish Yourself

Use the next two pages to research and write down a whole load of healthy recipes and foods that you can easily prepare for yourself to eat. There's also space for a shopping list so you can list any ingredients that you want to buy to prep your selected meals.

SHOPPING LIST:

Final word: ditch the word "diet" from your vocabulary. Replace "diet" with words such as "fuel", "nourish" and "enrich". By starting to see wholesome food as something that is going to add power, vitality and gold-dust to your warrior body, you'll feel more motivated to reach for the good stuff.

Go Dancing

Physical movement, once you're used to it, is an incredible mood booster. It makes your body strong, will upgrade your self-image, help fight off depression and arms you with immunity against illness. When you do something active happy chemicals are unleashed in your body: serotonin and endorphins. Together, they'll get you fired up, feeling good and ready to take on the world.

Side note: If you're not used to doing sports or you haven't exercised in a while, getting started can be a real mission. The thought of getting hot, sweaty and panty is not the most appealing idea to your sense of relaxation.

I get this.

Comfort zones and duvet days are seductive, however, your body was **made to move**. This flesh-and-bones outfit that you inhabit is a living, breathing gladiator that requires training and movement to access its true power. Once you're used to moving more, accustomed to a raised heartbeat and your lung capacity has improved, you won't look back. I promise.

Here are a few tricks to go from a non-sporty, couch-potato-princess to a body-loving, maven of movement:

 USE IMAGINATION. Think about your favourite action-film heroes and imagine that you are one of them. For example, you know the heroine from your favourite zombie film? Did she get bad-ass with an inactive gym membership? No. She got out, got dirty, ran away from zombie hordes and sweated – a lot! Pretend you are her and go and do your thing.

USE FRIENDS (in a good way!). Meet a friend so you can get started and get motivated together. Make each other accountable for what you're going to do and push each other on if one of you gets seduced by the sofa. Also, find activities that are uber cool. Everyone likes to have a few bragging rights and being able to say you're now a surfer, martial artist or super-bendy Yogi are all added bonuses for your personal brand.

 USE ADVENTURE. Your journey into movement is a great way to bring some more adventure into your life. You may not be old or rich enough to go backpacking with your besties this summer, but trying out classes and groups can add a different sort of spice to your life. Dipping your toe into a load of different classes means you'll get active and also have more chance of finding the activities that you really enjoy.

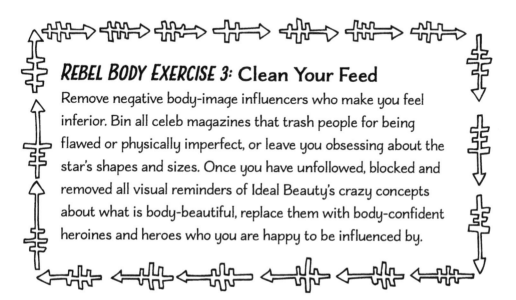

REBEL BODY EXERCISE 3: Clean Your Feed

Remove negative body-image influencers who make you feel inferior. Bin all celeb magazines that trash people for being flawed or physically imperfect, or leave you obsessing about the star's shapes and sizes. Once you have unfollowed, blocked and removed all visual reminders of Ideal Beauty's crazy concepts about what is body-beautiful, replace them with body-confident heroines and heroes who you are happy to be influenced by.

Body Language

Your body talks. Your body is literally communicating how you feel inside. From the moment that you wake up in the morning to the moment that you go to sleep, the way you move, sit and stand is a physical manifestation of how you are feeling inside.

Think about some of the confident people at your school.

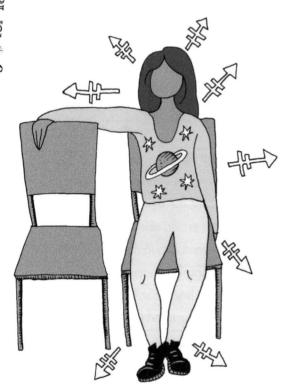

They explode into the classroom, throw themselves down into their seats, sprawl their legs and throw their arms outwards. They take up space and make their presence felt. On the other hand, consider someone at your school who isn't very confident. They hide their body behind folded arms, hug their books to their front, hunch their shoulders and look down, generally making themselves look small.

Studies have shown that when a person feels confident, they tend to stand, sit and walk in a particular way. It doesn't matter about their gender, age or nationality, studies show that big, expansive body language gives the message that a person is full of confidence, personal power and self belief.

These same studies also demonstrate that when a person isn't feeling good about themselves, their body language closes in and contracts. They tend to cross their ankles, fold their arms, press

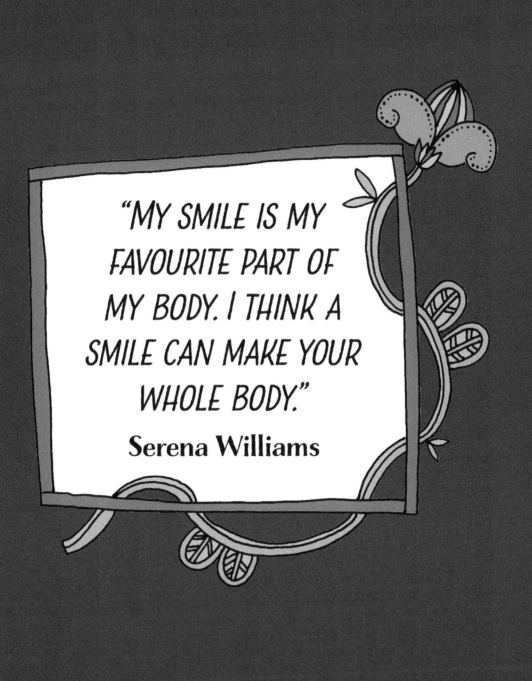

"MY SMILE IS MY FAVOURITE PART OF MY BODY. I THINK A SMILE CAN MAKE YOUR WHOLE BODY."

Serena Williams

REBEL BODY EXERCISE 4: Inspire Your Fire

Find images that represent the way you want to feel when you are fully strong, healthy, vibrant and amazing in your own body. Stick these images all over the page below and overleaf, then rip it out and stick it onto the fridge to remind yourself of who you are and why you want to enrich your body with everything it needs, both in terms of nourishment and movement.

Your Body, Your B.F.F

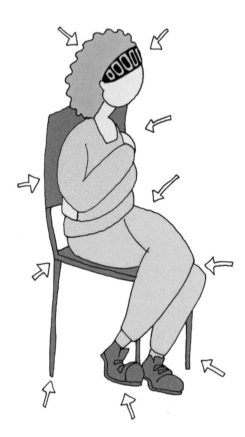

example, if you stand in small, timid postures, people will think you must be a small, timid person. This results in you feeling even more insignificant. On the other hand, when you stand in a confident way, you'll generally feel more powerful, projecting an image to others that you have high self-esteem and strong self-belief. Again, people who witness this unspoken message will treat you as someone who is worthy of their attention.

Over recent years, researchers and scientists across the world have been fascinated by the subject of body language and have undertaken many studies on the subject. Some of these studies have suggested that it isn't just other people who make assessments about us based on how we stand or sit. They say that there's another person who is continually observing and watching how we are holding our physical selves. Any idea who that is? Yep: **YOU**.

Social scientist, Amy Cuddy, proposed in her 2010 TED Talk, that when people hold their bodies

their hands against their faces and touch their necks a lot. When someone holds themself in small, disempowered postures, they communicate to others that they feel weak, uncertain and incapable.

Onlookers can read your body language. They observe what your body language is saying about you and then they treat you accordingly. This creates a domino effect. For

REBEL BODY EXERCISE 5: Are You Sitting Comfortably?

Stop reading and take note of how you are sitting right now. Are you crunched up, back hunched and ankles crossed? Or are you spread out, open limbed and relaxed? The posture of your body right now is telling the world who you are and how you feel. Which message do you think you're putting out there? Write your answer below.

------

in expansive postures, hormones are released that increase that person's feelings of confidence, self-assurance and personal power. She added that when a person holds themselves in a small, disempowered pose, a hormone is released that makes that person feel insecure and anxious. Based on her research, Cuddy suggested that if a person is feeling nervous or worried and they hold themself in a power pose (see opposite) for 2 minutes, that the hormones released will help the person start feeling much more confident and empowered.

This means that by simply changing the way you are sitting or standing, you can turn a valve that switches on your biggest, boldest, most brilliant confidence.

REBEL BODY EXERCISE 6: Power Up Your Pose

Check out the poses on the page opposite. Stand up, shake your arms and legs to wake them up and try standing or sitting in the different poses. Make a note of how you feel in each posture. In the space below, write down the points in your day or week when you feel nervous or low in confidence. How could shifting your body language change that?

Pose 1: ....
....

Pose 2: ....
....

Pose 3: ....
....

Pose 4: ....
....

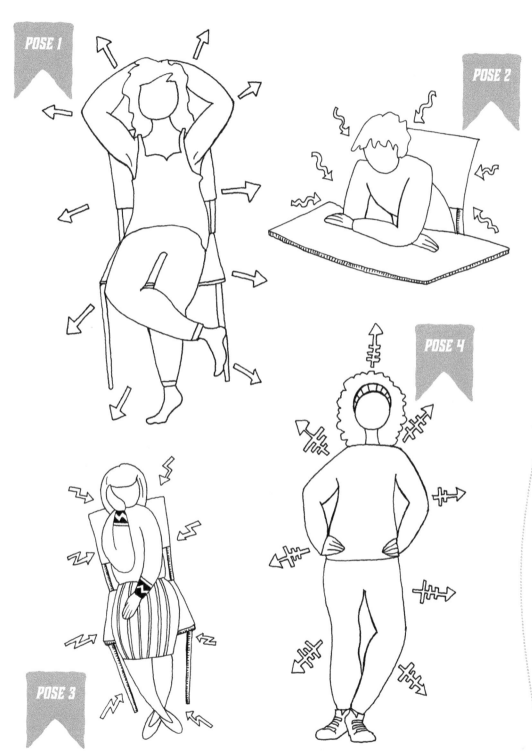

POSE 1

POSE 2

POSE 4

POSE 3

Body Labels:

A major reason that girls often have disempowered body language is because they are trying to hide parts of their body that they don't like. People suck in their tummies, wrap themselves up in layers of clothes and walk in ways that hide their perceived "bad bits". This not only plays havoc with our body language, but it is also a massive drain on our energy.

As an example, I recently worked with a young lady called Gemma. At the time, Gemma had been seeing her boyfriend for five months. During those five months, Gemma told me she had noticed that one side of her face was more attractive than the other. She became increasingly paranoid about her boyfriend seeing her "bad side" and so had spent their entire relationship positioning herself so that only her "good side" was visible to him. This involved her spending huge amounts of time and energy always making sure she was sitting, walking or standing on the right side of him, and making sure only one side of her face was ever photographed. By the time Gemma came to see me for coaching she was exhausted, suffering from anxiety and hugely paranoid that her boyfriend would notice her "bad side" and think she was unattractive.

Whilst Gemma's story is an extreme example of how people try to cover up their perceived body flaws, many of us will identify with doing this a little bit. For example, have you ever put a cushion over

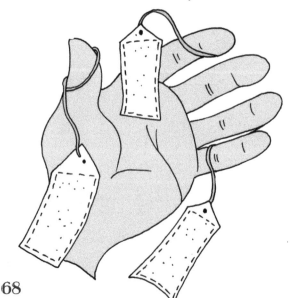

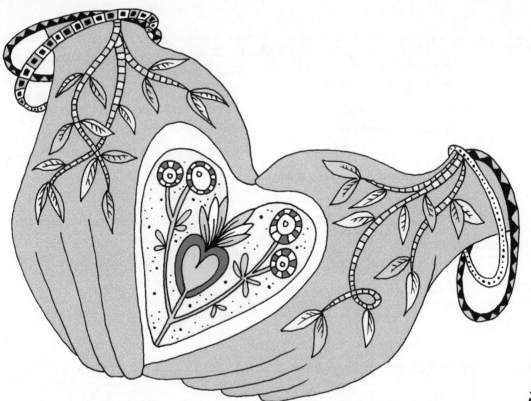

your lap to hide your stomach when sitting down? What about stooping your shoulders to try and make yourself look shorter? Or perhaps folding your arms over your chest to conceal your boobs?

One easy way of freeing up our bodies from weird contorted ways of walking, sitting and standing, and liberating it into free, open-armed gorgeousness is by taking some time to explore how you've labelled your body (both positive and negative, see p.70) and then upgrade those body labels. By body labels, I mean the ways that you secretly describe your body parts.

For example, when I was little, my mum pointed out how large and square my hands were. She compared my "builder's hands" to my cousin, who had long, tapered fingers that were perfect for playing the piano. For many years after that

69

I felt really self conscious about my hands. I'd hide them inside my jumper sleeves and avoided pointing or doing anything that would draw attention to their chunky appearance. By hiding my hands up my sleeves, I gave off the message that I was nervous, timid and withdrawn with my body language.

Over the years of growing my gorgeousness, however, I started to see my hands differently. I realised that not everyone has hands that can draw like I draw, or plant gardens or create beautiful calligraphy and handwriting. My hands are incredible, unique and talented. As a result of changing my perception of my hands, I no longer hide them away. My hands confidently point, express, gesture and communicate what I want them to communicate.

REBEL BODY EXERCISE 7: Rewrite Your Labels

Use the space opposite to write a sentence about each of your body parts and the words you use to describe them. E.g. Legs: thick, shapely, chunky. Eyes: pretty, dark, smiley etc. Now look at your body through Rebel Beauty Eyes. Think about how those sentences can be improved. Be creative in your new descriptions. E.g. Hands: Creative, gifted, able to touch the world. Rewrite your labels.

The body you conjure up with your strong, empowered descriptions is your Rebel Body. How does it feel to see yourself through these positive eyes? Does looking at your body positively change the way you want to treat your body? How?

_____

_____

_____

_____

_____

_____

_____

_____

_____

_____

_____

_____

> Your Body, Your B.F.F

REBEL VOICE

Word Up!

Do you ever worry about what other people think of you? Does keeping quiet and biting your tongue feel easier than opening up and telling people what you really think? Have you ever swallowed back your feelings with friends, only to take those feelings out on someone else, say your mum or dad, later?

If you have ever felt small, unheard, overlooked or are frequently bending yourself into all sorts of contortions to accommodate other people, the chances are that you need to do some Rebel Voice training.

As children, most of us are brought up to be "good". We are encouraged to put people's needs before our own and look after others' feelings. While this is a brilliant way of making sure humans grow up to be kind and supportive, few of us are taught how to also respect our own feelings and boundaries.

Imagine you have a friend who always lets you down, fails to turn up or blabs your deepest secrets to anyone who will listen. Now imagine that you don't tell your friend that their behaviour upsets you because you're worried about having an argument. Initially, you might feel better keeping your mouth shut, pretending you're not upset and trying to ignore what's happening, but after a while you'll notice that this method of communication has some pretty funky side effects:

 Your feelings build and you start to dislike your friend, driving an invisible wedge between you.

 You feel weak and self-critical for lacking the courage to speak up.

 You start to feel inauthentic and untruthful in that person's company.

 You lie awake at night playing out arguments in your head, as you think of all of the ways that you could tell your friend what you really think.

 Your feelings start to fester, you get snarky and you take it all out on unsuspecting loved ones.

 Eventually a teensy-tiny thing triggers you and you have a massive blazing row with your friend. The level of anger you feel is disproportionate to the minor thing that they've done, but it's the build-up of EVERYTHING that is now exploding from your mouth like a red-hot volcano!

REBEL VOICE EXERCISE 1: Face Your Fears

As you'll find out in the rest of this chapter, there are cool, collected ways to express what you're feeling and still walk away with your dignity and relationships intact. But, before we move on, here's your chance to brain dump any fears you might have about being true to **YOURSELF**, by completing the sentences below:

If I were to tell people what I really feel, I might...

If I were to tell people what I really feel, they might...

The thing that scares me most about telling people what I really think is...

In the past when I've tried to tell people what I really think or feel, this is what happened...

Does any of this ring a bell? It doesn't have to be like this. Having the courage to know yourself, know your needs, speak up and walk **YOUR** talk is a vital part of nurturing your gorgeousness. It means that you value, like and respect yourself. The more you can get into the habit of listening to your inner voice, accessing how you feel and valuing those feelings by letting them be heard, the stronger you'll feel and the more you'll like who you are.

At the same time, the idea of expressing your true feelings to people might feel butt-clenchingly scary. You might have a bad memory of trying to stand up for yourself. Perhaps you had a massive argument and got really upset. Maybe you got tongue-tied and felt humiliated. If this is the case, remember that the past and the present does not equal the future. Yes, telling the truth about your feelings can be uncomfortable at first but your feelings are also worth fighting for.

Communicating:
The Icky Way

Sometimes the best way to work out **HOW** to do something, is to first work out how **NOT** to do it, right? Let's take a quick look at the icky cycle that most people seem to follow when communicating.

1. Expectation

We all have expectations. It's a unconscious inclination that comes to us more naturally than gobbling up freshly cooked chocolate-chip cookies. For most of the time we're blissfully unaware of our expectations... that is, until the thing we expect to happen doesn't. For example, we all wake up in the morning and expect our rooms to still be there. But, imagine waking up and looking around to discover that half your house has fallen through a sink hole. Your expectations would be rudely interrupted!

2. The painful "TING" of disappointment

When people walk around with multiple expectations it's inevitable that sometimes these expectations will be unfulfilled. There are a whole host of different feelings that can be triggered when expectations aren't met. Some people will feel anger, upset, sadness or maybe even betrayal, but underlying most of these is a core feeling of disappointment. Imagine that you arrange to meet up with your B.F.F on Saturday morning for a shopping trip. You're excited to meet up (expectation) but they ring you at the last minute to say they're cancelling. Or maybe they don't ring and just fail to turn up at all. How would that feel? Upsetting? Possibly. Disappointing? Definitely!

3. Zipped lips

Faced with unfulfilled expectations, many people will bury their feelings and zip their lips. Yes, they might feel disappointment, but because most of us have been taught to think of other people's feelings before our own, they would be unlikely to say anything.

Think again about the example of your friend cancelling an arrangement at the last moment. If they'd never cancelled on you before, you'd possibly say, "No dramas! It's fine. We can do it another time." You'd swallow back your feelings, withdrawing your feelings of disappointment. But if your friend had cancelled on you lots of times before and you'd already pretended it was okay and not said anything in the past, all those buried feelings would start to bubble to the surface and be much harder to ignore. When feelings of disappointment build up they can quickly start to multiply and turn from disappointment to feelings of anger and resentment.

4. Hiding from icky feelings at all costs

The trouble with a build-up of aggro is that, even if we pretend we're not feeling it or swallow it back, it's still there, swirling inside us and making us feel anxious, up-tight and angry. Like a toxic dog fart trapped in your room, if you don't open the windows to release the stale air, that pong isn't going anywhere!

A common way that humans try to avoid painful feelings is to distract themselves with temporary feel-good fixes, that are often far more harmful than we realise. These fixes might come in the form of:

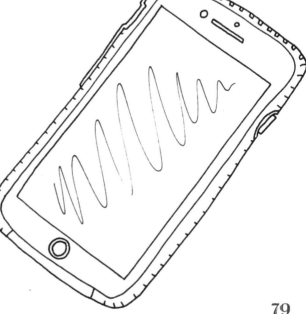

 Endless social media scrolling

 Taking bazillions of selfies

 Binge eating all the chocolate biscuits in the house

 Smoking

Self harm

 Over-exercising

 Drugs or alcohol

None of these substitutes will help you deal with the feelings that you're trying your best to swallow down. Once the initial release they offer has worn off, or you're no longer engaged in doing them, the same feelings will be waiting at the back of your brain, ready to pounce! Prolonged use of escape methods such as these can lead to addiction and serious health problems. That's why suppressing your feelings isn't healthy and simply doesn't work.

5. THE RAGE!

Eventually, when enough negative emotion has been swallowed down and built up inside you, it all comes together and explodes out as THE RAGE! Every bitten tongue, every polite smile to say, "Don't worry. It's fine" builds up into a great hot fireball of emotion that could explode from you at any moment.

So, that friend who keeps making arrangements and breaking them? Imagine they are late again, this time to meet you in the school canteen. You find that,

try as you might, you can't swallow down any more disappointment and this one tiny act is enough to trigger anger of Hulk-like proportions. Your friend looks at you and is like, "Why is she so angry all of a sudden?" She has NO IDEA that your anger is the build-up of countless disappointed expectations.

6. Emotional splurging

The outcome of exploding feelings will be different depending on what the situation is. Chances are, you'll have a big row with someone and once you're finished being angry, you'll cry and then break down and tell them all of the things you've been holding onto for all this time. Every hurt and disappointment will come rolling out in a sticky, snotty, tearful pile. If that person loves you and is kind, they will listen to what you're saying, hear your upset and respond accordingly. Sometimes though, big rows don't get sorted because no one is sure how to communicate properly (did I mention most of us are clueless about how to express our feelings). It might be that the build-up of resentment that you've been storing inside you has damaged the relationship irreparably. Whether the relationship with that person continues or not, if you continue withdrawing communication in your relationships, this cycle of ickiness will continue indefinitely.

Most people spend their whole lives locked into this churning cycle of feelings and actions. At first they bury their emotions in whatever route of escapism gives them a momentary release, but over time feelings build and they get THE RAGE and splurge their feelings all at once. Repeating the same cycle over and over again.

REBEL VOICE EXERCISE 2: Own Up to Your Ick

What's your usual mode of communication? What do you do to avoid your feelings if you're upset? Do you recognise your own behaviour in the icky way of communication? Use the box below to list the "icky" ways that you recognise from the way that you have communicated with people in the past.

Communicating: the Rebel Voice Way

Thank your lucky stars that **YOU** are not going to get trapped in this cycle of Ick! Why?

Because you, my friend, are a rebel. You are different. You are about to reverse the norm and become a master of your own voice, communication, relationships and destiny. You're going to learn how to deliver your feelings with power, precision and clarity. No freak-outs. No splurge. Here's how:

Word Up!

1. Expectation

Sorry, but there's no quick fix here - your expectations aren't going to go away. Even after you've unleashed the full power of your gorgeousness, you're still going to expect things to happen. It's a basic human instinct that we've all gotta live with.

2. The painful "TING" of disappointment

And if you're still having to live with the weight of your expectations, you're still going to suffer disappointment. The sad fact is that

people are going still let you down...
Your bestie will still "forget" to return
the make-up she borrowed, your
mum will still take your sister's side
in an argument. Basically, there will
always be things that wind you up
and you're still occasionally going to
want to withdraw inside yourself and
let those feelings of disappointment
fester.

3. Rebel Voice

BUT instead of withdrawing
communication and going quiet,
bingeing out on escape routes or
getting THE RAGE, this time you're
going to unleash your Rebel Voice.
Here's how:

 Trust that it's okay to feel what you're feeling. The worst thing to do
with feelings is resist or bury them. Take a deep breath and make a
note of the sensations that these feelings trigger in your body. Maybe
try journalling and expressing that feeling in words. Or, try drawing
the feeling as a picture or symbol.

 Once you're ready to talk to the person who has disappointed
you, start off by explaining to them the FACTS around what
has happened. Describing the facts is clever because it means that
you aren't accusing the other person. Instead you are highlighting
the truth as you both understand it, i.e. "We had made an
arrangement to hang out on Saturday and then you messaged
and said you couldn't come."

Once you've described the facts, explain how those facts made you
feel. This way you are not accusing the other person and triggering
their defences, but simply explaining how the situation made you
feel, i.e. "I was really gutted when our arrangement was cancelled
because I'd been looking forward to it all week."

♥ Now comes the hard bit. Listen to what the other person has to say. I mean REALLY listen. Stop thinking about how cross you are and hear their side of the story. They may apologise, realising that you're upset. They may explain what happened, for example. "I had a massive argument with my boyfriend and needed to sort it out" or "my little sister is being bullied and I needed to spend time with her."

It may be that the other person ends up revealing something that you could never have expected. For example, perhaps they suffer from really bad anxiety and sometimes find it hard to leave the house, but have been too afraid to admit it. Or they might just have let you down for no good reason at all.

♥ Work out what you want. There is always a chance that the person you are talking to doesn't "hear" how you are feeling, ignores the situation or gets defensive when you talk to them.

Take your friend who cancelled that arrangement on Saturday. If they listen to what you've told them and still don't change their behaviour, or have no valid reason as to why they're letting you down, you need to decide if you are prepared to continue making plans with them. Is this person really worthy of being your friend? On the other hand, if the friend explains they have anxiety and struggle with going out, or had a family crisis to deal with, think about how could you both move on from this? Maybe you would be happy to go and hang with her at her house instead?

♥ Move on. Walking away from a conversation that has allowed you to express your truth, keep your cool and direct it with clarity and purpose is the most empowering feeling, and the more you do it, the easier it gets. Even if the other person hasn't fully "heard" you,

you've still witnessed and validated your own feelings by acting on their behalf. Knowing your feelings and needs are witnessed and validated by YOU is a massive step forwards in building your confidence, self-esteem and all-round gorgeousness.

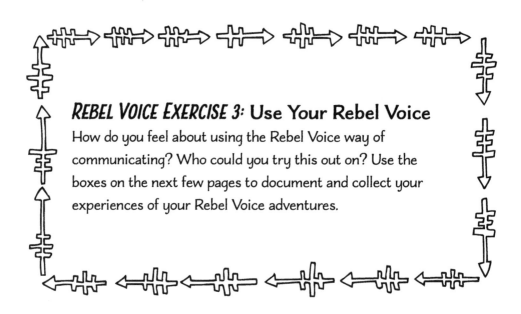

REBEL VOICE EXERCISE 3: Use Your Rebel Voice

How do you feel about using the Rebel Voice way of communicating? Who could you try this out on? Use the boxes on the next few pages to document and collect your experiences of your Rebel Voice adventures.

THE SITUATION WAS...

MY EXPECTATIONS WERE...

I WAS DISAPPOINTED/LET DOWN BY...

I RESPONDED BY...

THIS HAPPENED AS A RESULT...

WHAT I'LL DO DIFFERENTLY NEXT TIME...

Word Up!

THE SITUATION WAS...

MY EXPECTATIONS WERE...

I WAS DISAPPOINTED/LET DOWN BY...

I RESPONDED BY...

THIS HAPPENED AS A RESULT...

WHAT I'LL DO DIFFERENTLY NEXT TIME...

THE SITUATION WAS...

MY EXPECTATIONS WERE...

I WAS DISAPPOINTED/LET DOWN BY...

I RESPONDED BY...

THIS HAPPENED AS A RESULT...

WHAT I'LL DO DIFFERENTLY NEXT TIME...

Word Up!

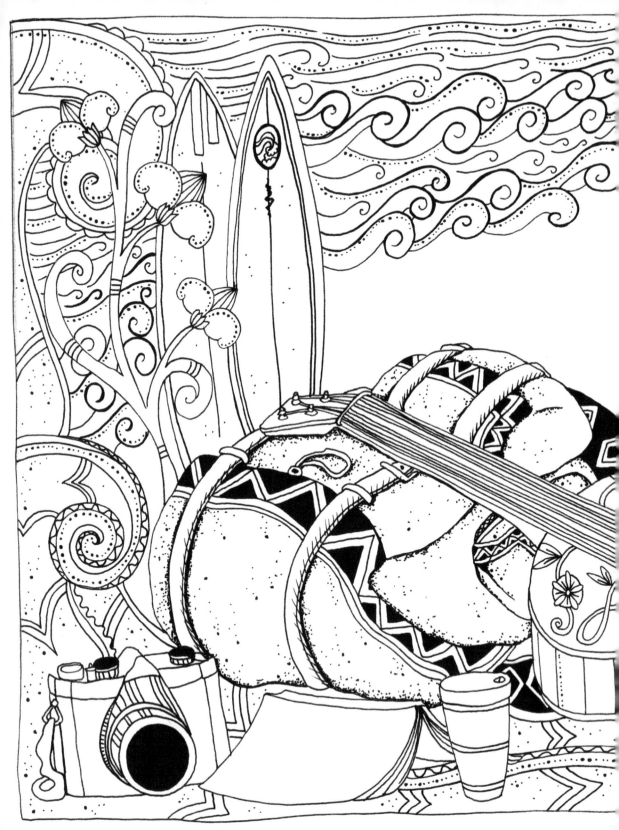

REBEL PASSION

Find Your Zone

Passion. It's the thing you love; the activity, music, person or place that powers you up, makes your heart sing and has your mojo doing a double-dive back flip.

Passion is like a little fire that exists inside each of us and is fueled by our own uniqueness. What makes one person say "WOW!", may seem crazed, quirky and off the wall to someone else. For example, right now I am ridiculously into kick-boxing and Japanese sword fighting, whereas you may find yourself salivating over cooking an authentic Italian ragu or have a burning crush on a folk guitar player from Alaska.

Our passions aren't static, but are in a continuous state of movement and growth.

Sometimes we'll go through passion dry-spells, when our inner flame is wavering and we wonder why life feels a bit bleurgh, but with a little bit of exploration, new adventures and horizon broadening, that flame will come back stronger, sparkier and more powerful than ever.

REBEL PASSION EXERCISE 1: Find Your Spark

Circle any of the words below that spark your interest and give you a sense of excitement. These are just a starting point, so feel free to come up with your own words if you prefer.

Art

Food

Adventure

Film

Animals

Drama

Travel

Culture

Music

Online

Theatre

Now write a little sentence to expand and deepen into what you specifically love about those things you have circled. Chances are that just by thinking about the things you love in life and the world, you'll be grinning on the inside very soon.

Your Passion, Your Happiness

By now you've probably realised that the world we live in has got a lot of stuff back to front and inside out.

We're told that we'll find happiness when we buy a certain item, when our body looks a certain way, when we end up with a Hollywood acting career or when we're so rich we can buy a luxury private jet for every day of the week and have a garden big enough to store them in. The challenge with pinning your happiness on something outside of yourself is that you can never be sure that the thing you are focused on will actually bring you that happiness.

However, if you focus inside of yourself and find the activities and experiences that set your unique heart on fire and bring these things into your life as much as possible, **YOU** become the person who determines your happiness.

Right now, some of you will be like, "I have NO idea what my passions are!"

To you, I say this: most teenagers go through a few years of struggling to work out who they are and what they like. Some adults even backpack around India, doing mountain top yoga retreats or running ultra marathons through desserts to try and "find themselves".

REVELATION: the place you need to look to find yourself, find your passions and capture your unique gorgeousness isn't up a mountain, or half-way along the Great Wall of China. Your self is right here, right now, inside **YOU**.

Everything you're ever going to learn about yourself is always going to happen right here - inside your own subjective experience. If you have the confidence to trust in yourself and start opening your mind to new things, ideas, subjects and stories, at some point your inner flame is going to flare up and light you up from the inside.

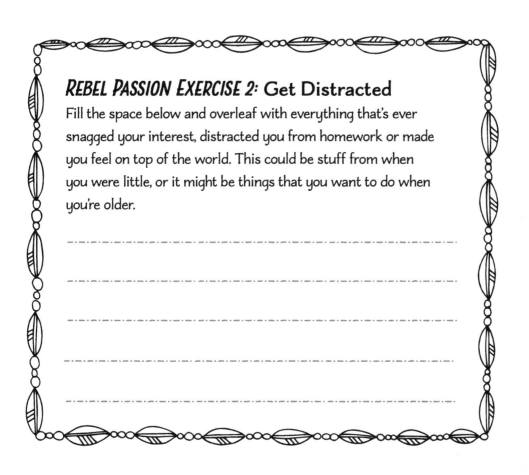

REBEL PASSION EXERCISE 2: Get Distracted

Fill the space below and overleaf with everything that's ever snagged your interest, distracted you from homework or made you feel on top of the world. This could be stuff from when you were little, or it might be things that you want to do when you're older.

Your Passion, Your Gifts

Sometimes our passions can act as helpful signposts that direct us towards a future career or job. For example, if you go gooey over writing, maybe you could lean towards a future in publishing or journalism. Or, if you're passionate about make-up, hair and history, perhaps you could find a career working backstage doing the hair and make-up for actors and actresses who star in period films.

Even if you don't think you're particularly good at the thing you love doing, when you're passionate about it, nothing else tends to matter. The bottom line is that if you enjoy doing something so much that you'll go back to it again and again, you won't be able to stop getting better at it. Eventually, you're going to shine.

Weirdly, if we're really miserable in some way, this can also direct us towards our true passions. The environments we find ourselves in will often make us feel a certain way, and if you hate where you currently are, the chances are that what you truly love is not in that place.

Take Tulisa. Tulisa hated school. She found lessons boring, sitting still was unbearable and all she wanted to do was get out of the stuffy classroom and go outside. Without really taking the time to understand her, her teachers labelled her as naughty and disruptive, yet countless detentions and trips to the Head-of-Year's office had no effect on her behaviour.

Tulisa came to me for some coaching and after chatting to her for a while, she began to tell me about her horse. As Tulisa described how much she loved riding, being at the stables and around the animals, getting her hands dirty by mucking out the horses and the volunteering she did on an equine programme, a whole different light seemed to shine from her. She was vital, alive, in the zone and passionate. Her eyes glittered and she was suddenly a fountain of knowledge and enthusiasm.

"You do realise what this means?" I said.

"What?" she asked.

"Tulisa. You are a horsewoman. You need to be outside with horses. This is your passion and this is what you need to do to thrive and shine."

Tulisa went on to do an apprenticeship at a nearby equine centre and never looked back. Her teachers were relieved and, with her passion ignited, her focus in the classroom improved. It wasn't that Tulisa was bad or naughty, but the environment of school just didn't suit the unique, talented individual that she was. Her true passions and gifts were situated elsewhere. When she was allowed to express that aspect of herself, she thrived beyond belief.

REBEL PASSION EXERCISE 3: Looking Forward

Imagine it's the future and you've managed to sculpt this incredible life in which you get to pursue all of the things you love. Answer the questions below in turn, to add some colour to your dream life.

1. Where do you wake up?

2. What is the first thing you do when you wake up?

3. Who do you have around you?

4. What are you wearing?

5. How will you spend your morning?

6. Where will you eat your lunch and what will you have?

7. How will you spend the afternoon?

8. How will you spend the evening?

9. What's the highlight of your day?

10. What is the feeling you get from this life you've created for yourself?

Now draw a picture of you living your life based upon your passions. How would you feel? What would the aesthetic of your life be? What theme would your life have? What would you be surrounded by in the picture?

Your Passion, Your Gorgeousness

How does it feel when you're totally absorbed in something you love doing? Do you lose awareness of what's going on around you? Does time seem to speed up or slow down? How do you feel in your body and self when you're in "the zone"? Imagine if you could bottle that feeling and access it whenever you want.

The sensations and feelings you experience when you're in "the zone" are completely unique to you. The way you describe those feelings are as individual to you as your fingerprints. It's this combination of feelings that we're going to call your "gorgeousness" – your unique feeling of beauty – and it's those feelings we are now going to capture so that you can access them wherever and whenever you want.

You're probably wondering, "How on earth do you catch a feeling? It's not like I've got a magical net that allows me to capture the feels like they're butterflies!"

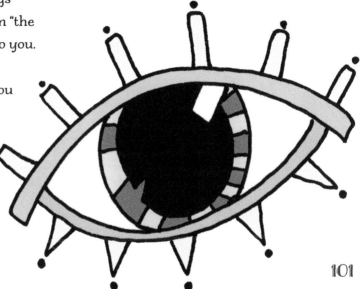

The answer is that you're going to capture your feelings by using one of the psychological techniques that's helped Levi's, Coca Cola and Netflix become some of the biggest brands in the world.

Build Your Brand

A brand is an identifying symbol, mark, logo, name, word or phrase that companies use to distinguish their product from others. Thanks to widespread marketing, we know hundreds of thousands of brands. We may think that we don't really notice them (let alone get influenced by them) but because of the way that our unconscious mind locks onto the imagery, fonts and emotional suggestions of a brand, they influence us WAAAAY more than we think.

By using words and symbols that are meaningful, familiar and attractive, brands are able to embed their product's identity deep into our unconscious minds. Through the use of TV adverts, visual images in magazines and carefully curated scenes that tap into our inner desires, companies are able to attach strong emotional triggers to their brand and products. For example, a drinks company might show lots of images of cool hipsters hanging out on a beautiful sun-drenched beach, drinking their brand of cola. The images are designed to trigger our inner desires of belonging, freedom, acceptance and popularity. Basically, we want to be those hipsters ourselves.

Result?

We, the viewer, unconsciously associate those feelings with the brand and the combination of strong visual and emotional associations, leads us – the customer – into going out and buying the product. It's this emotional relationship we build with brands – and their logos – that makes them so powerful.

Now imagine designing your own branded logo that triggers your best feelings of happiness, beauty, contentment and confidence. Imagine that every time you looked at that image, you were able to access feelings of empowerment and gorgeousness that you usually only get if you're immersed in doing something that you truly love.

Imagine that, eventually, all you have to do is visualise that logo in your mind and wherever you are, whoever you're with, you could feel that sense of connection and gorgeousness filling you up. Sound good? Great, because that's exactly what you're about to do.

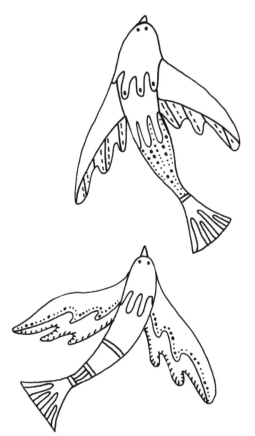

Step One: **Visualise**

Your brain might be clever, but funnily enough, it can't tell the difference between whether you are doing something or simply imagining yourself doing it. For example, if you visualise yourself in a happy place, doing stuff you love, you'll naturally begin to summon those inner feelings of happiness and contentment. Put this book down, set an alarm and spend five minutes imagining yourself doing the thing that you love, whether that be hanging with your friends, listening to music, dancing, designing t-shirts, whatever. When your alarm goes off, open your eyes and move onto the next step.

Step Two: **Capture**

In the box below, write down everything you felt when you were doing the visualisation. How did you feel physically in your body? Light, relaxed, energised? What did you feel emotionally? Free, happy, excited? Now that you've written down how you felt, distill those feelings into seven words and write them in boxes on the opposite page. If you're struggling to think of words, check out the examples at the top of the opposite page to see if some of them might be suitable. Make sure you have seven strong feeling words.

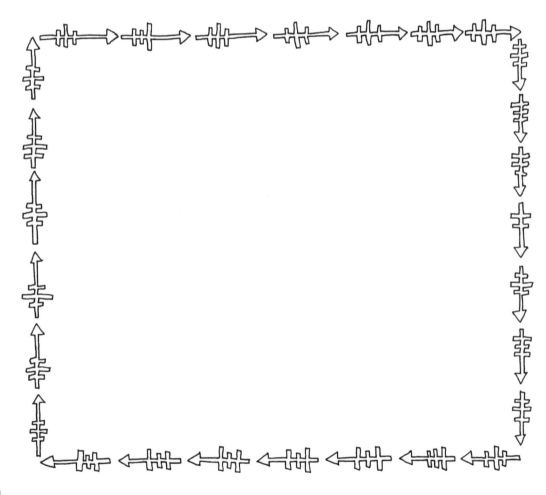

Caring Real
Vibrant Assertive Sassy Funky
Confident Loved Brainy Sensitive
Exotic Strong Kind Aligned
High-flier Smart Honest
Clever Respected Unique Fit Charged
Adventurous Powerful Cool Flowing
Spiritual Unique Unusual Soft Funny
Successful Knowledgeable Abundant Healthy
Elegant Natural Friendly Creative
Thoughtful Independent Thoughtful

Write your seven words
in these boxes:

Step Three: Draw

Now that you've got your seven words, draw seven corresponding symbols to represent those feelings in the box below. These pictures don't need to works of art. As long as you know what they mean, that's all that matters. If you struggle, a good way of thinking up symbols is to attach the feelings they evoke to an animal. For example, if your wrote "freedom" maybe draw a bird. If you wrote "powerful", you could draw a lion. Make your symbols simple and add lots of colour.

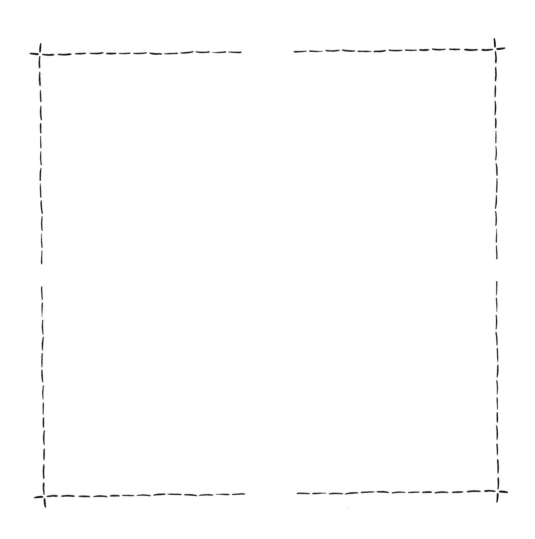

Step Four: Brand

This is where the biggest companies in the world have drawn their magic from: the visual image. Your job now is to combine all seven symbols you've created into one image. Use the space below to let your creativity go wild. Connect all the symbols up. It doesn't matter if it looks weird, or even if you have to alter a few symbols to make them work. Once you've created your brand image, add in more colour. Your unconscious mind is drawn to colour, so the stronger the visual image, the better it will lock into your brain.

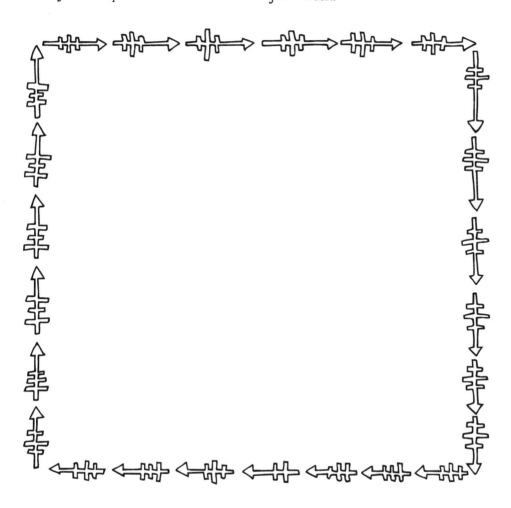

Step Five: **Absorb**

In order to make this brand work its magic and trigger your feelings of gorgeousness, you need to train your brain to associate the image you've created with the feelings you experience when immersed in your passions. Once your mind makes the association, simply imagining the image should help you to feel positive, confident and beautiful.

Question: How do you train your brain?

Answer: You need to look at your brand each day, reminding yourself of the feelings that are locked into it.

It has been said that it takes 21 days to form a new habit. How can you commit to looking at your gorgeousness brand for 21 days? Could you put it on your phone as the screen saver? Could you photocopy it and stick it on your wall? Whatever it is, each time you look at your gorgeousness brand, remind yourself of all those positive feelings. Perhaps even imagine you are in your "zone" so those feelings get summoned into your body as you gaze at the image. Do this as much as you can, but at least once a day.

REBEL PASSION EXERCISE 4 : Putting Your Passion into Play

Write down any ways you think your life would change for the better if you could bring your Rebel Passion feelings into your day more. How would your home life shift? How would your happiness levels grow? Would school, friendships and your ideas about the world and your future begin to change?

REBEL POWER

Crown Your Cycle

You've spent hours agonising over it with your bestie. Cringed when your science teacher talked about it in class. Wondered when you'll eventually get it... and speculated about who has theirs already. Then, one day, you go to the loo, notice blood in your undies and you realise **IT** has finally happened. Gulp.

YUP, YOUR PERIOD IS HERE.

In this life-changing moment, it's only natural that your brain will be churning with thoughts and questions.

"OMG, is that blood?"

"OMG, does this mean I'm now a woman?!"

"OMG, how do I actually use this sanitary towel thing? Should it feel like I'm wearing a nappy?!"

Getting your first period is a rite of passage. You've stepped through a door into womanhood and there's no going back. Scary, huh? It really doesn't need to be. Once you've had your first show of blood, it can take several months for your

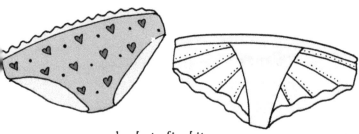

body to find its rhythm, but don't worry, eventually your body will settle into a monthly cycle and you are likely to bleed every 28 days or so. Some people's cycles are shorter and some are longer, so if your cycle isn't 28 days long, don't panic.

After the initial drama of getting your first period has passed, other questions and realisations may start to kick in. For example:

"Holy heck, does this mean that if I have sex, I'll get pregnant?"

"Oh god! I've come out without my pads/tampons. What do I do if my period starts unexpectedly?"

"Oh no. I'm due my period and am meant to be going to the beach. Should I cancel?"

Though you've probably been thinking about getting your period for years, once it does arrive it can come as a bit of a shock to realise that you're going to be negotiating this monthly visitation - and its impact - for the next 40 years of your life! If you listen to messages in the mainstream media, you may feel that having a period is a bit of a curse, however, there's another way to look at your cycle that offers a very different story. In fact, it's the key to unlocking your innate female super power.

Crown Your Cycle

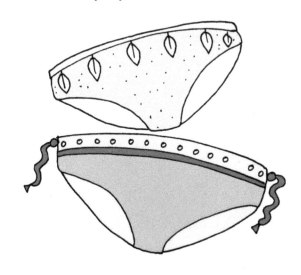

REBEL POWER EXERCISE 1: End of story. Period.

Use the box below to write down your period story. Has it happened yet? If so, how did it happen? Where were you and how did you feel? How do you feel about periods now? If yours is yet to come, are you nervous? Are periods your friend, frenemy or foe?

Whatever your relationship is with your period, the reality is that you're just at the start of your journey and you're going to be living with it for a long time yet. Everyone experiences their periods differently, but whatever your experience is, you're likely to spend a lot of time doing at least some of the following:

 Working out when your period is going to happen.

 Feeling like you want to crawl into bed and stay there all week, eating nothing but chocolate.

 Experiencing period pains and funky hormones shifts (pre-menstrual tension).

 Watching annoying TV adverts that show you all the things you can't do if you're on your period and all the things you CAN do if you use the advertiser's menstrual products.

 Going to a party you've been looking forward to for ages and wearing your favourite dress, only to spend most of the evening panicking that you may leak on it.

Based on the above, it's kind of easy to see why many people spend their menstruating years hating their periods. Yet, your period is way more than P.M.T. chocolate cravings and backache. It is actually part of a much larger cycle that – if understood – can help you to power up your work, studies, friendships, self-esteem and creativity.

I know this is hard to believe, but stick with me for the...

Big Rebel Power Reveal

So, here's the thing, most people think that women have a week of bleeding and then go back to their lives. Most people are **WRONG!**

In truth, the female body is constantly whirling around in a big, hormonal state of flux. Every 28 days our mind and body boogie between different phases, stages, chemicals and hormones. With each of the stages that you move through during the menstrual cycle, you will feel, act and perceive your live and self in a different way. Crazy, huh?

For example, during ovulation your hormones can have you feeling like you're Queen of the Universe. You may make plans to go out partying, message all your friends and even people you'd normally be too shy to chat to. You may come up with incredible ideas for projects and feel indestructible on every level. But then, a few days later, when you're no longer ovulating and the hormones in

your body have started to take a down-turn, self-doubt can start to kick in. You might look at your diary and facepalm when you see all of the events you scheduled when you were full of confidence a few days before. Suddenly, the former Queen of the Universe (you) skulks into her bedroom, creeps under the duvet and wants nothing more than to binge on box-sets and chocolate, and to never have to speak to another soul ever again. Is that too much to ask?

These changes in your moods can make you feel a bit inconsistent and irrational. If you're unaware of how your hormones are impacting on your moods and outlook, you'd be forgiven for thinking you were, in fact, crazy. However, when you begin to understand the language of your body's hormonal happenings and learn how to ride the waves of your menstrual cycle (both the ups and the downs), you'll start to realise that there is, in fact, a clear

pattern to it all. And not only can this pattern be tracked, it can also be used to help you level-up every area of your gorgeous life.

Menstrual Geekery

Your cycle and how you feel within each phase of it is unique to you. When you understand how your feelings and outlook change as you move through the month, you'll be able to make plans tailored to your mood and energy ahead of time, look after yourself and understand your unique quirks in a whole new way.

For example, once you know you are ovulating, you can use this powered-up time for dynamic activities such as partying, making new connections and letting out your inner-diva. You will also know not to let this Queen of your cycle dictate your entire diary, because you'll know that a week later you may not be feeling quite so dynamic. You can then use your quieter "inner" times for major self-pampering, chilling at home with your journal or chaining the latest much-watch box-set.

On the next few pages, you'll be taken on an exploration of the four stages of your menstrual cycle: pre-ovulation, ovulation, pre-menstrual and menstruation. Each of the stages will be broken down into the following sections:

1 **Body Lab** - where you will find out what is happening at a chemical level in your body during that stage of your cycle.

2 **Inner Feels** - the possible emotional side-effects that are likely to kick in during each hormonal phase.

3 **Outer Actions** - to-do lists aligned with each phase.

Just remember, your cycle is as unique as you are! These are guidelines, not hard and fast rules, so don't be surprised if you experience things a little differently. At the end of this section you will find the **Rebel Power Trackers** which will allow you to keep track of each stage of your cycle and how you experience it. Armed with that info and the guidance on the following pages, you will be able to understand and predict the way that you'll be feeling as your monthly cycle progresses – predicting the highs and the lows before they happen and harnessing all your unique power as a result!

The Four Phases of Your Cycle

Pre-Ovulation
(days 7-13)

Body Lab

Ovulation is the part of your cycle when an egg is released from one of your ovaries. **Pre-ovulation** is the bit in your cycle **BEFORE** ovulation happens. At this point of your cycle, your bleed has finished. You may not know it, but the hormone **oestrogen** has started to increase and this, in turn, boosts the **serotonin** - feel good chemicals - in your brain. As you move further into your cycle, another chemical, **testosterone**, increases, giving you a friendly boost of strength, motivation and confidence - fuelling you with extra mojo for your actions and activities. Whoop!

Inner Feels

Thanks to the boost in oestrogen and serotonin, your energy and enthusiasm will start to boost in the days that follow your period. With oestrogen climbing higher, you'll probably begin to feel bolder, braver and up for any challenge. Your mood will be upbeat and you'll be more likely to want to be around people. The chances are you'll also feel more self-assured about your appearance. In fact, weirdly, at this time in the cycle, a woman's attractiveness is boosted by subtle shifts in the soft tissue in her face, making features appear more symmetrical.

Outer Action

New, fresh, full of potential and possibility, your enthusiasm to go out, meet friends and interact with the world will be overflowing. Your verbal skills will be sharp, making it easier to chat, socialise, make important calls and (shudder!) even do public speaking. This is a great time to get creative and start new projects, start going to the gym again, learn new things and meet new people. If you begin to experience anxiety during this phase, yoga, hot baths, brisk walking and meditation can help reduce any hormone-fuelled angst.

REBEL POWER EXERCISE 2: Take Note!

Start a journal specifically to capture what you're thinking and feeling during your menstrual cycle. Use the page below to get started, but you may want to spread your wings and use a pad or notebook to give yourself space to express yourself.

Ovulation
(days 14–21)

Body Lab

Hola ovulation! As mentioned in the previous section, this phase of your cycle is when a tiny egg is released from one of your ovaries in preparation for making a baby - yikes! Since the beginning of your cycle, your oestrogen and testosterone have been working as a biological power-team to gear you up for getting preggers. All of that super-confident, upbeat energy is a cunning plan of your body's, aiming to attract a mate. During this phase, if you have sex and don't use contraception, the chance of getting pregnant is at its highest.

Inner Feels

Chances are you're not planning on baby making, but your biology doesn't know that. What you can do instead is use all of this super-fertile, creative energy to bring projects, ideas and goals to life. Your power to make and create is cranked up to high octane and whilst also pumped up on happy hormones, you'll have the strength, dynamism and self-assurance to push these projects through. So now is the perfect time to get creative!

Outer Action

This is a point in your cycle when you'll feel most productive, capable and

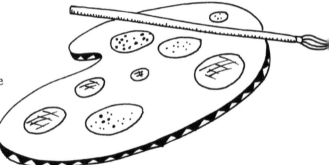

collaborative. Use this to smash the to-do lists. Verbal skills will be heightened to the max, so it's a great time to see people, have conversations, network, audition for performances and bring your full expression into the world.

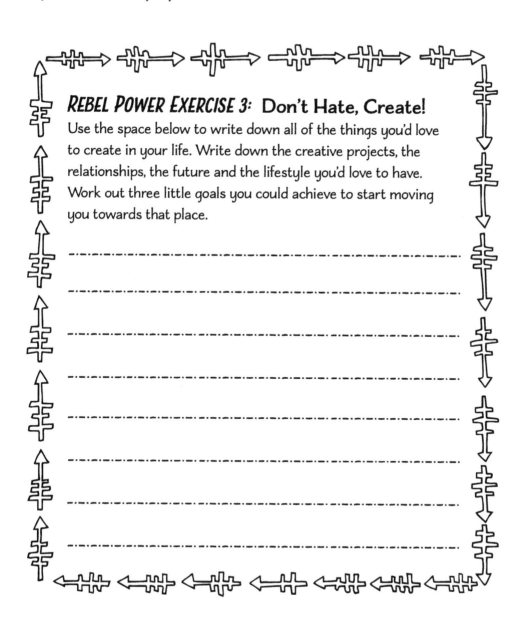

REBEL POWER EXERCISE 3: Don't Hate, Create!

Use the space below to write down all of the things you'd love to create in your life. Write down the creative projects, the relationships, the future and the lifestyle you'd love to have. Work out three little goals you could achieve to start moving you towards that place.

Pre-Menstrual (days 22-28)

Body Lab

The pre-menstrual or "luteal" phase of a woman's cycle, tends to have a bad rep. Your oestrogen, testosterone and progesterone hormones start to plunge. This sudden drop in oestrogen can create feelings of nervousness, anxiety and tearfulness. Decreasing serotine and the return of noradrenaline, means that if something irritates you, you're likely to snap. Withdrawing progesterone can leave you crying at anything and decreasing testosterone leaves you with those creeping feelings of self-doubt. Meanwhile, the **corpus luteum** (the matured egg) dies and the uterus lining disintegrates. During this time you may get fuller breasts and a bloated stomach due to fluid retention.

Inner Feels

Shifting hormones during this phase may have you feeling emotional, tired and restless. Tolerance for annoying situations and people crashes. Every irritating thing you've glossed over during the rose-tinted ovulation days, becomes glaringly obvious - and you probably won't be shy of asserting yourself to tell people about it! You might experience tearfulness, grumpiness, lady rage or your inner critic going wild and pointing out everything that's rubbish about the world/your life/you. This probably leaves you wondering how the heck we can use this part of our cycle for positive action!

Outer Action

Your pre-menstrual phase is the "truth phase" of your cycle. It might feel painful and sometimes irrational, but honoured for what it is, the pre-menstrual stage can serve as a powerful "life edit" tool, helping to clean up areas of our home, relationships or personal habits that aren't working for us. Because of your sharpened eye for detail, this is also a great time to do accounts, proofread documents and get all those loose ends tied up.

It's important to know that your eye for detail can spy the flaws in your life, self and others. Instead of turning on anyone, write down the things you think need changing and then put them to one side to reassess during a different part of your cycle.

Side note: Drink water. By drinking lots of water, we flush our bodies through, wee a lot and therefore helps to reduce water retention.

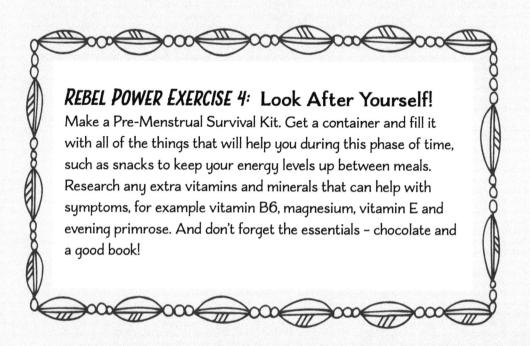

REBEL POWER EXERCISE 4: Look After Yourself!

Make a Pre-Menstrual Survival Kit. Get a container and fill it with all of the things that will help you during this phase of time, such as snacks to keep your energy levels up between meals. Research any extra vitamins and minerals that can help with symptoms, for example vitamin B6, magnesium, vitamin E and evening primrose. And don't forget the essentials – chocolate and a good book!

Menstruation
(days 1-7)

Body Lab

The first day you bleed is day one of your menstrual cycle, marking the very beginning of the new cycle. If you haven't started already, THIS is the day to begin charting your cycle. If you're not preggers, your uterine lining (now disintegrated) is being released in the form of blood. Hormones are at rock bottom, the lowest levels we experience for the entirety of our monthly cycle but your oestrogen is beginning to climb again. By day three you'll begin to experience a lift in your mood and energy. Don't get too excited though as everything is still pretty low, so on these days you're likely to feel called towards rest and self-care.

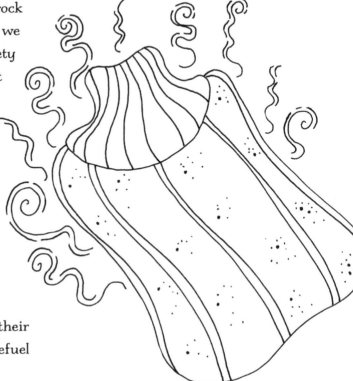

Inner Feels

During Winter months, humans tend to retreat, hibernate and generally want to get cosy. Exactly the same is required of women during the menstruation phase of their cycle. Use this time to refuel yourself, find time to relax, create space to read a book and practise gentle self-care. Most girls don't get stomach cramps for the first few years of their periods. Later on they may get pains, which can feel like a dull, squeezing ache in the lower tummy area. This is the result of the uterus squeezing to help the blood come out. Period pains can be really uncomfortable and are part of the reason why our "Inner Winter" has a bit of a bad reputation.

Outer Action

Here are a few ways that you can deal with the pain of periods:

- Exercise, such as walking and swimming are great as they don't put too much stress on the body.

- Relaxing activities, such as taking a hot bath, meditating or a warm water bottle or wheat bag on your tummy can help ease discomfort and offer relief from painful cramps. Gentle yoga can also help, though make sure you speak to your yoga teacher to find the right exercises. Stretching in the wrong way could make pains worse.

- Doctors sometimes recommend going on the contraceptive pill if the pain is very bad, as this can make the period less heavy and lessen the horrible achey feeling. If you're period doesn't give you discomfort, honour this part of your cycle by laying low, chilling out and taking it easy as much as possible.

REBEL POWER EXERCISE 5: Be Prepared!

Make a period box (for home) and period bag (for away). In your box (for home) place period products (tampons, sanitary towels, moon cups), chocolate, book and a blanket. In your bag (for away) put period products (tampons, sanitary towels, moon cups), baby wipes or tissues, emergency knickers and a few small, brown paper bags so that you can easily dispose of your used pads or tampons if a bin isn't in reach.

Track Your Cycle

Now you have a clearer idea of your hormonal landscape, how do you start connecting with your Rebel Power and understanding your unique cycle? Using an app or calendar to track your cycle is a great way to record your dates and let you know when you can expect your next period to arrive. If you're into bullet journaling, this is also a fab way to track your dates... But I'd like you to take this a step further.

Instead of just working out when you're due to bleed, why not begin tracking how you feel on each day of your monthly cycle? Once you've done this for a few months, you'll be able to look back and see if any patterns are emerging. For example, on day 23 you might find yourself feeling really disconnected from your friendship circle, or just feeling sad for no real reason. If you then look back at day 23

from the month before and see that you had similar feelings on those days, it would suggest that this feeling is the result of your hormones shifting. Realising that you felt the same way last month at this time can be reassuring. It means that you can mentally step back from your negative emotions, recognise that the feelings are likely to be connected to your hormonal changes and, instead of reacting to those feelings (such as ditching all of your friends and resolving to become a hermit), you can practise some gentle, loving, self-care instead.

As you notice the patterns in your cycle, you'll find that it is easy to embrace the times when you're rocketing upwards hormonally. But learning to love yourself when you're feeling cranky and wiped out is an equally powerful part of growing your gorgeousness.

REBEL POWER EXERCISE 6: Keep Track!

Use the trackers on the following three pages to capture your mood on each day of your cycle. Start on day one (the first day of your next period) and each day write three words to describe your mood. Continue doing this for the next three months, then look back to see if you can see a pattern in your moods and feelings. For example, maybe you'll discover that on day 13 of your cycle, you often feel upbeat and outgoing but on day 18 your mood dips and you feel less sociable. Once you start finding these regular mood patterns in your cycle, you begin to know what to expect during each phase – and then have the knowledge and power to look after your needs more.

The grid tracker on pages 134–5 allows you to note the date that your period comes each month and also to gather info on how it shows up. On the first day of your next period, mark the date on the tracker. Also, fill in the key at the bottom of the tracker to come up with a colour code to denote whether your flow was light, medium or heavy, then use this key to fill in the tracker. Finally, mark if you experienced any cramping. As you use this tracker month on month, you'll be able to see whether your periods are regular or irregular. You'll also work out how many days long your cycle is, meaning you'll (hopefully) know when to expect it each month.

Start Date ....

Cycle 1

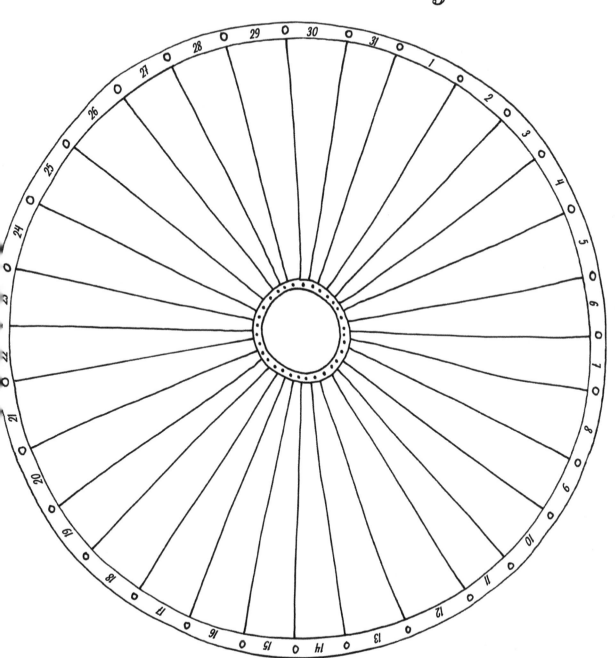

Cycle 2

Start Date ....

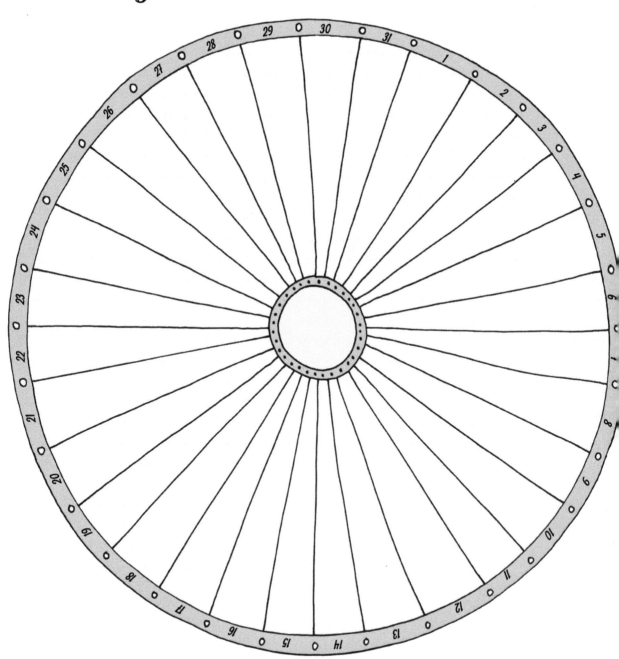

Cycle 3

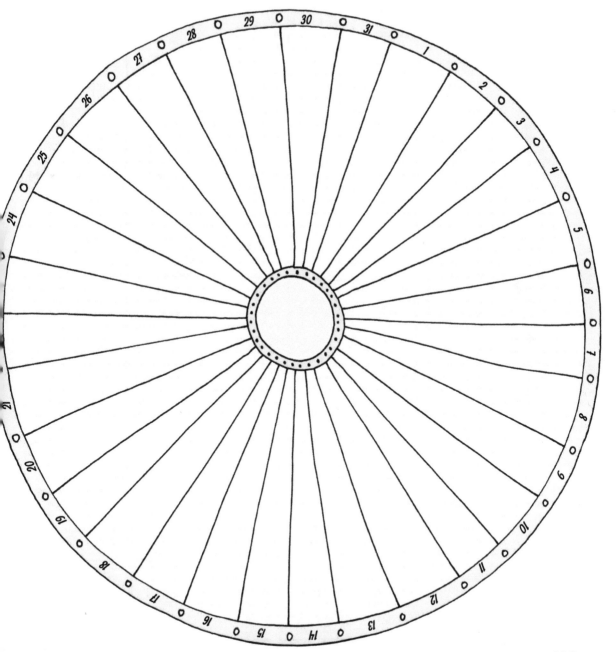

365-Day Period Tracker

	1	2	3	4	5	6	7	8	9	10	11	12	13	14	15
JAN															
FEB															
MAR															
APR															
MAY															
JUN															
JUL															
AUG															
SEP															
OCT															
NOV															
DEC															

LIGHT

MEDIUM

16	17	18	19	20	21	22	23	24	25	26	27	28	29	30	31

HEAVY ☐

CRAMPING ☐

REBEL PURPOSE

Finding Your Way

When I was 5 years old, I exploded into my family's kitchen and slapped a scrappy, hand-drawn book I'd been making down onto the counter.

"I'm going to be a writer," I told my dad, excitedly. "And I'm going to write books that change the world."

"Change the world in what way?" asked my dad.

"Saving the rainforest?" I said.

My dad nodded. "Good plan."

From that moment onwards, the compulsion to write – and to try and change the world with my writing – has never left me.

Between the ages of 7 and 12, when I was bullied about how I looked, I wrote books. During my teens, when I suffered from an eating disorder, dropped out of school, left home and hated how I looked, I continued to write. Even when I had nowhere to live, no money to buy food and no idea which direction to take, my pen still scribbled on paper. Sometimes I'd write poetry, other times I wrote pages in a journal and a lot of the time I wrote short stories and mapped-out novels. Now, 35 years later, I'm still putting pen to paper, but these days I write exclusively about how people can grow their gorgeousness, develop self-love and live more creative lives. I can happily say that I've finally achieved the goal set by my 5-year-old self of writing books that help the world in my own special way. YAY!

But, make no mistake – this is freaky behaviour. Most adults have **NO** clue what they're going to do with their lives, let alone sticking to a plan they made up at 5 years old. In fact, many people get halfway through their careers and still have no idea if they're on the right path or not. Students are expected to make choices about studying subjects and make important decisions about their future at a time when they're still unsure what their favourite crisp flavour is. And all of this confusion is exacerbated by the lives we see projected through social media, where influencers and celebrities seem to be touched with the sparkling fairy dust of life purpose and higher destiny.

How is it that they have already found their path and why does it all unfold so easily for them? Is it because they were born under the star sign of Leo with their rising sign in Scorpio? Is it fate? Is it destiny?

NOPE. It's none of the above.

As human beings we each have a set amount of undetermined time to live our lives. During our time we will do some stuff. Some of the stuff we will do will be worthwhile and helpful. Some of the stuff we do will be less

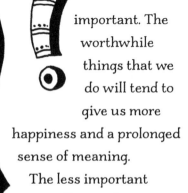

important. The worthwhile things that we do will tend to give us more happiness and a prolonged sense of meaning. The less important stuff – watching soaps, scrolling screens, stalking frenemies – is padding.

So, when you're asking the big philosophical questions (and as a Rebel Beauty Teen, you **will** ask big questions) and you're staring out of the window and sighing, "What is my life purpose? What am I here for?" maybe try asking yourself some different questions. For example, "What is important to me? How can I use my time to do something worthwhile?"

These, my friend, are way more powerful questions. Here's why:

♥ These questions are time-saving. You're less likely to waste precious hours searching for the "meaning of life" on the internet and falling down endless rabbit holes that will lead you everywhere from flat-earth theory to astrology, from religious cults to free online tarot websites and all sorts of other sleaze and cheese as a result.

♥ These questions are answerable. People can waste their entire lives wandering around in circles hypothesising about their grand, higher purpose here on planet Earth and then getting endlessly frustrated when it doesn't show up wearing feathers and unicorn glitter, slapping them on the shoulder and shouting, "Hi, it's me!".

♥ These questions are practical. By asking yourself what you can do with your time that is worthwhile, you can get off the sofa and discover what feels good to do. You can find out what you consider important and then work towards that.

So, let's ask them. Ready?

REBEL PURPOSE EXERCISE 1: Choose Your Path

Answer the questions below and on the following page as quickly, slowly, simply or as in-depth as you wish.

What is important to me?

How can I use my time to do something worthwhile?

_____

_____

_____

_____

_____

_____

_____

_____

Ultimately, only YOU can discover what is important and feels purposeful to you. Actually going into the world and finding those things is the best way that you will find meaning and a sense of purpose in your life. The more you start to explore this – and the more you tune into what feels important to you – the more your actions will become informed by those callings and, before you know it, you'll be living a life of meaning and purpose.

Finding Your Rebel Purpose

So, now that you are no longer sucked in by the robotic clutches of Ideal Beauty and instead have an armoury of gorgeousness to unleash in the world and make it a better place, how do you get started? After all, let's face it; your bedroom is comfortable, the TV is seductive and endless YouTube videos are just a thumb press away. Getting started on changing the world first requires finding the things that really call to you. This involves digging deeper into that first question, "What is important to me?" A calling is an issue or injustice that, like a hook, snags something deep inside your heart or mind and keeps tugging you towards focusing on it. For example, a calling could show up as:

 An issue in the world or your community that really winds you up, makes your blood boil, your teeth grind and won't let you shake the feeling. Let's be honest here. You only have to watch the news to see that it is glaringly obvious that the world has one or two problems. It needs all the helping hands it can get. What is the issue that stands out to you and makes you want to do something to change the world?

The issue that used to really wind me up was the impossible beauty standards that are forced upon us by the media and cosmetic industries. I believe that people who are preoccupied with being physically "perfect" are accidentally cheating themselves and the world out of their true greatness and potential. My frustration with this issue led me to write my first book, **Grow Your Own Gorgeousness**, which was later developed into a school programme and has now helped countless girls to reclaim their bodies, disentangle themselves from Ideal Beauty and develop their own Rebel Beauty instead.

A nagging idea, plan or project that you're convinced could help improve a situation in your community, in

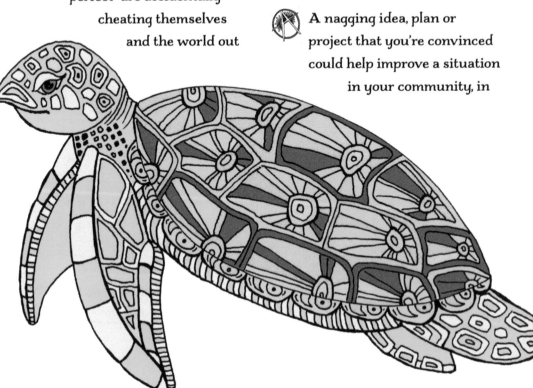

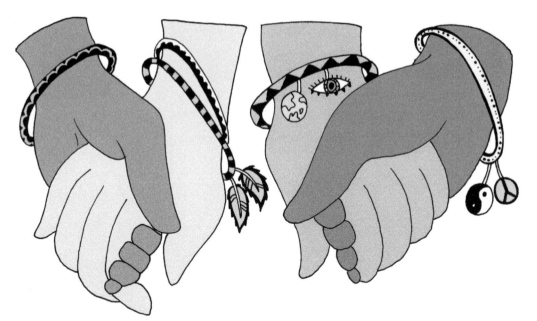

nature or for people in the wider world. You find yourself daydreaming about doing it, you talk about it with your friends and you feel a strange sense of ownership over it. It's as though YOU were born to offer the solution. To do what you are called to do may take a lot of effort, but it inspires and motivates you on every level. If you could come up with or contribute a solution to any world issue, what would you want to help sort out and how would you want to do it?

 You have an idea of something that would give your life a sense of meaning and purpose. You aren't sure if you have the character, confidence or resources to do what you are planning, but none of that is going to stop you. It's not about making money or getting more friends or a popularity contest... you are called to do this thing because JUST DOING IT would feel so rewarding.

REBEL PURPOSE EXERCISE 2: Take Issue

Write down anything you have seen on the news or in the media that annoys you. Why does this upset you? How does it make you feel? What would you love to do to change it?

Once you've worked out what cause you want to support and add your voice to, the next step in changing the world and walking your path of purpose, is to answer the second question, "How can I use my time to do something worthwhile?" This involves, well... **getting involved**.

For example, if you're anxious or upset about the amount of plastic in the sea, maybe you could join a beach clean or organise some sort of sporting event to raise awareness of single-use plastics? If you're appalled by deforestation in the Amazon, perhaps you could do a sponsored activity to raise money to help the World Land Trust

purchase and preserve acres of jungle in that area. Perhaps a poster asking for volunteers catches your eye each time you go to the shops – well, this is a perfect time for you to put your hand up. Callings come in all shapes and sizes and it's your job to hear them and respond with actions that you believe are important and worthy.

Have a think about whether there is any voluntary work you could do to support your cause.

Which fun, brilliant project could you start to raise awareness about the thing you're trying to change? Is there a fundraising activity could you do to raise money for a charity you believe in?

REBEL PURPOSE EXERCISE 3: Picture-Perfect World

In this box, draw a picture that illustrates the world in a way that you would like it to be. For example, if you love the environment, draw nature thriving. If you would like to see sanitary products given freely to women in developing countries, maybe draw people from an organisation distributing these products. Start clarifying and visualising the world you want to see in your future.

REBEL PURPOSE EXERCISE 4: How Can I Help?

Write down what you would do to help, even if you weren't paid to do it. Brain dump all the ways you could tie your passions in with the thing that you'd like to change in the world. For example, if you love music, could you put on a performance to raise some funds? If you're an artist, could you make posters that raise awareness of an issue you feel strongly about?

REBEL PURPOSE EXERCISE 5: Stop the Press!

Imagine you are in the future and a newspaper or magazine reporter is coming to interview you about something totally AMAZING that you have done. Write the article below and on the next page. Cut it out of this journal, sign it, fold it up and put it away to open 20 years from NOW.

Become the Change You Want to See

Whilst having a grand vision to change the world is epically cool, we don't actually have to become Boudica-style protesting eco-warriors or women's right activists to have a worthwhile impact on the world around us. By making small changes to the way you live each day, you can go to bed at night knowing that you've quietly changed the world. Mahatma Gandhi is believed to have said, "Become the change you want to see in the world". By this he meant, that if you want to see friendship in the world, be a good friend. If you want to see truth in the world, be honest. If you want to experience love in the world, be as loving as you can be.

Here are some suggestions as to how you can **be the change:**

 Be a leader: Great people, great acts and great things are often unique and unconventional. To achieve those things, we need to go against the herd mentality, which can be scary. The risk of feeling like an idiot is part of the pathway toward doing meaningful things, but you can choose to have the courage to stand up for what you believe in. Be the person who says "Hi" and welcomes in the new kid.

153

Be the person who refuses to talk badly about her body and instead points out the things that she loves about the way she looks. Be the person who knows her Rebel Beauty and isn't afraid to lift others up and let them see their own gorgeousness too.

Be a trend-maker: We can all sit around and wait for the people in our families or communities to make small changes, but someone has to start the trend. Go to a garden centre, buy seeds and begin growing some of your own herbs and vegetables. Even if you only start off with some basil growing on your windowsill, your salads and pizza will taste amazing. Recycle and re-purpose your old things and make them beautiful again. Switch off lights when you leave a room, use energy-saving bulbs and research other ways you can save energy in your house and make your own living more sustainable.

Be kind: Smiling at your elderly neighbour as you walk down the street costs nothing. Paying a compliment to your friend, or saying "Thank you" to the person who served you in the shop are tiny acts of kindness that spread positivity and goodness in the world. Releasing a bee or spider from your house may seem like nothing, but each of these acts builds up your identity as being a solid, self-assured and fundamentally good human being who contributes to the whole. Acts of kindness spread happiness and make the world a better place – even if no one else is watching.

REBEL PURPOSE EXERCISE 6: Enforce Positive Change

List three things you'd like to see more of in the world. Examples could be peace, forgiveness, fun, laughter, connection, belonging, loyalty, honesty or kindness. Once you've written your three words, write down three ways you could change your behaviour to see more of these things on a day-to-day basis.

_____

_____

_____

_____

_____

_____

_____

_____

REBEL PRACTICE

Practice Makes Perfect

So far in this journal, you've learned six ways to help you see, act, speak, do, perform and be your most gorgeous self.

Now that you're better equipped at seeing yourself with **Rebel Eyes**, cultivating your **Rebel Body**, using your **Rebel Voice**, engaging in your **Rebel Passions**, deepening into your **Rebel Power** and finding your **Rebel Purpose**... I have a bit of a confession to make.

YOU'RE GOING TO FORGET EVERYTHING.

Yep. That's right. You're going to go back to judging yourself against Ideal Beauty. You're going to hate your appearance. You're going to mess up your communications, forget to live passionately, ditch the idea of charting your cycle and feel hopeless about your future.

But then, at some point, you'll remember the stuff in this book and you'll come back to it. And at that moment you'll need a strategy. You'll need a way to bring small, micro-movements into your day-to-day living so that you become really good at embodying your true gorgeousness. Gradually, each day, these little steps and movements forward will become habits and routines that you don't even realise you're doing. You'll have found your Rebel Beauty Practice.

Your Rebel Beauty Practice

Okay, think about something you're really good at. Perhaps you're a great swimmer, a talented artist or brilliant singer. If you can't think of anything, consider the fact you've learnt to walk, talk and use a mobile phone. How did you get to become so good at these things?

If I were to guess, I'd say that the reason is because:

A **You really wanted to do it.**
B **You tried it out.**
C **You practised.**

For example, you weren't born able to sing your favourite band's entire back catalogue, right? You heard the songs and they sparked a feeling, so you learnt a few words, hummed the tune and began to remember the lyrics. Eventually the songs became embedded in your mind. You also weren't born knowing how to walk, talk, hold a fork or play the guitar... You learnt these skills by practising.

Whatever you fancy achieving in your future, whether it's a health, hobby or career goal or unleashing your gorgeousness and living your best life, it's the daily habits – your practices - that you do regularly that build up and will eventually get you there.

That is why creating a Rebel Beauty Practice is important. By having a series of little actions that you can easily take each day, your habits will change and you'll eventually become more and more confident at being YOU.

So, if you are up for forgetting everything you've done and heading back to the ways of Ideal Beauty for a bit, then fold down the corner of this page and put this journal somewhere that you can find it in the future. Or, if you're up for starting a Rebel Beauty Practice that will help you to continue growing in your brilliance, boldness and beauty TODAY... Let's begin!

Creating Your Rebel Beauty Practice

A Rebel Beauty practice is a well-prepared plan that you put in place so that each day you're able to connect with and nurture your unique gorgeousness. Your practice will consist of the things that you can do on a physical, emotional, mental, social and purposeful level that will help to maintain and continue growing a beautiful, empowered YOU.

Whether you're going through the best time of your life or a crisis has hit, you can return to these practices day after day and reconnect with the qualities and value of your unique you-ness.

Use the next few pages to reconnect with each of the six Rebel Beauty steps. Each step will help you come up with an action that you can begin practising and tracking on the following pages.

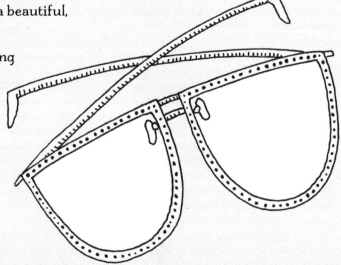

Rebel Eyes

How you see yourself defines how you behave and who you become. You have the power to choose what to focus your attention on. Write in the box at the top of the following page three words that describe how you want to see yourself in the next three months.

The Practices

♥ Begin a daily gratitude journal. Every day write down where you have experienced those qualities that you want to see in yourself. You might write down the names of people, things you've seen in the news, or times when you yourself have displayed those qualities. As you build upon this practice day after day, you'll begin to naturally find the gorgeousness that was there in you – and the world - all along.

♥ Look back at your answers to exercise 2 in the Rebel Eyes chapter (p.35) and write a list of 21 tiny steps you could take towards overhauling and improving them. Take one little action every day to help you learn to love yourself.

♥ Once a day, stand in front of the mirror and "see" yourself through the eyes of someone who loves you. This might be your best friend, a relation (or perhaps even your pet hamster!) Make a mental note of all the ways that individual might describe you.

Choose just one of the practices above, or come up with your own, and write down in the box overleaf what you're going to bring in as your Rebel Eyes practice.

This is the practice I'm bringing in to develop my
Rebel Eyes: ....

....

....

....

This is the time of day I'll do it: ....

Rebel Body

The more you value your body, the more you'll grow to love it and want to look after it. Cultivate your body love by bringing in movement, good food, empowering body language and positive body labels.

The Practices

Which one action could you bring in each day to help develop your Rebel Body? Come up with your own or pick from the options below:

 Eat a super healthy, power-packed breakfast. Or maybe walk to school instead of taking the bus? Body-love means nourishing your body with healthy food and movement.

♥ Use body language to improve your confidence. Which part of your day would most improve from positive posture and body language? Is there a certain lesson or time of your school day when you could do with a boost in confidence? If you choose body language as your daily practice, how will you remember to stand tall, pull your shoulders back and expand your zone?

♥ Remind yourself DAILY about your new, positive body labels. When you catch yourself feeling down about your body or comparing yourself to someone else, take out your list of body positive descriptions (p.70-1) and remind yourself of who you truly are.

Choose just one of the practices above, or come up with your own, and write down in the box below what you're going to bring in as your Rebel Body practice.

This is the practice I'm bringing in to develop my Rebel Body: ....

....

....

....

....

This is the time of day I'll do it: ....

Rebel Voice

A Rebel Voice doesn't necessarily demand airtime but it does mean learning to communicate your feelings, needs, expectations and boundaries. It's the tool you're going to need to fight your own corner and build the best relationships that you can have.

The Practices

If you're not already confident to voice your opinions or feelings, then try out some small micro-movements with this practice. Below are some simple ideas to get you started:

 Choose one person who you feel comfortable with and begin to practise the Rebel Voice way of communicating (p.83–9) with them.

 If you have a day where you feel triggered by something but are unsure what has happened, track back through your day until you find the point where you started to feel angsty. Was there an expectation that was disappointed in some way? Make a note of how you can use your Rebel Voice to communicate your needs.

 Each night before you go to bed, spend a moment visualising yourself speaking easily, fluidly and communicating your feelings kindly and respectfully to the people in your life.

Choose just one of the practices above, or come up with your own, and write down in the box at the top of the next page what you're going to bring in as your Rebel Voice practice.

This is the practice I'm bringing in to develop my Rebel Voice: ....

....

....

....

....

This is the time of day I'll do it: ....

Rebel Passion

Who you are and how you feel when you're engaged in your passions is the key to your unique gorgeousness. That sense of happiness, connection and flow is a feeling that you can cultivate in your life as much as you desire.

The Practices

 Every morning and every evening look at your Rebel Beauty Brand image (p.107) and connect with the feelings that you've embedded into the pictures. Feel those feelings and remind yourself of how it feels to be **YOU** at your best.

♥ Look at your diary and find a way to bring your passions into your day-to-day life at least four times a week. School, homework and other life-madness can take up a lot of space in the week, but there will always be a way to make time for the things that make your life feel good. Once you've scheduled these times into you diary, make a note of the days that you managed to do the things you love.

♥ Commit to delving more into your top-most passion. What one thing would help you to get even better at the thing you love the most? Are there any goals you could set around this?

Choose just one of the practices above, or come up with your own, and write down in the box below what you're going to bring in as your Rebel Passion practice.

This is the practice I'm bringing in to develop my Rebel Passion: ....

....

....

....

....

This is the time of day I'll do it: ....

Rebel Power

Women and girls are cyclical beings. When you tap into your body's cyclic code, you will begin speaking a language that only you and your body understand and uncover some new superpowers in the process.

The Practice

There is really only one practice for Rebel Power... and that is to chart your cycle. You may already have a charting app on your phone, but I'd also suggest writing three words a day in your journal (or use the trackers on p.131–5) that describe how you are feeling. This could be emotionally, physically, mentally, socially and so on.

 Use the Rebel Power trackers to capture three words a day to describe how you feel.

 After three months of charting your cycle, compare your trackers to see if any sort of pattern has emerged. Are there "black holes" that you fall down each month? Are there days when you're super excited about being alive and fill up your whole diary for the year?

 Begin tweaking how you approach your feelings each day, based upon your new knowledge of Rebel Power and new-found understanding of your own unique cycle.

Write down in the box on the next page how you are going to keep track of your cycle, whether using a smartphone app, a dedicated journal or the Rebel Beauty trackers found on pages 131–5 of this book.

This is the way I'm going to track my cycle: ....

....

....

....

....

....

This is the time of day I'll do it: ....

Rebel Purpose

A life that's rich with meaning and purpose tends to feel empowering. Even when crisis hits, when you have a sense of purpose you have the inner mojo to keep moving forward and power through to the other side.

The Practices

Keep your mojo pumping with some of the practices below:

 Stay connected to your purpose. Read books or articles, listen to podcasts and develop your ideas with up-to-date information about your particular purpose and calling. Knowledge is power.

♥ Take dynamic action towards your purpose. How can you set up micro-projects that contribute towards helping your purpose? For example, could you hold a cake sale at school to raise money for something? Could you volunteer at an organisation to help support a charity? Maybe you could write letters, set up a blog or join a group? Brainstorm all of the ways that you can take steps to support your purpose and, most importantly, follow through with these actions.

♥ Once a day, put your school, your parents and your peers aside for ten minutes and tune in to your inner self. Ask yourself, what do I really want? How can I spend my time on what I believe is worthy and important? What can I do right now to make a difference?

Choose just one of the practices above and write down in the box below what you're going to bring in as your Rebel Purpose practice.

This is the practice I'm bringing in to develop my Rebel Purpose: ....

....

....

....

....

This is the time of day I'll do it: ....

Rebel Eyes Practice:-

DAY		DID IT!
1		
2		
3		
4		
5		
6		
7		
8		
9		
10		
11		
12		
13		
14		
15		
16		

DAY		DID IT!
17		
18		
19		
20		
21		
22		
23		
24		
25		
26		
27		
28		
29		
30		
31		

Use the trackers on the next few pages to track and stay accountable for your Rebel Beauty Practices. Each one will help you keep track on one aspect of your practice for one month, so copy or photocopy the tracker before filling it in if you would like to monitor your progress for longer.

Notes & Reflections:-

....

....

....

....

....

....

....

REBEL BODY PRACTICE:-

DAY		DID IT!
1		
2		
3		
4		
5		
6		
7		
8		
9		
10		
11		
12		
13		
14		
15		
16		

DAY		DID IT!
17		
18		
19		
20		
21		
22		
23		
24		
25		
26		
27		
28		
29		
30		
31		

NOTES & REFLECTIONS:-

....

....

....

....

....

....

....

....

....

....

....

....

REBEL VOICE PRACTICE:-

DAY	DID IT!
1	
2	
3	
4	
5	
6	
7	
8	
9	
10	
11	
12	
13	
14	
15	
16	

DAY	DID IT!
17	
18	
19	
20	
21	
22	
23	
24	
25	
26	
27	
28	
29	
30	
31	

NOTES & REFLECTIONS:-

....

....

....

....

....

....

....

....

....

....

....

REBEL PASSION PRACTICE:-

DAY		DID IT!
1		
2		
3		
4		
5		
6		
7		
8		
9		
10		
11		
12		
13		
14		
15		
16		

DAY		DID IT!
17		
18		
19		
20		
21		
22		
23		
24		
25		
26		
27		
28		
29		
30		
31		

NOTES & REFLECTIONS:-

REBEL POWER PRACTICE:-

DAY		DID IT!
1		
2		
3		
4		
5		
6		
7		
8		
9		
10		
11		
12		
13		
14		
15		
16		

DAY		DID IT!
17		
18		
19		
20		
21		
22		
23		
24		
25		
26		
27		
28		
29		
30		
31		

NOTES & REFLECTIONS:-

REBEL PURPOSE PRACTICE:-

DAY		DID IT!
1		
2		
3		
4		
5		
6		
7		
8		
9		
10		
11		
12		
13		
14		
15		
16		

DAY		DID IT!
17		
18		
19		
20		
21		
22		
23		
24		
25		
26		
27		
28		
29		
30		
31		

NOTES & REFLECTIONS:-

....

....

....

....

....

....

....

....

....

....

....

Final Word

Did you know that the meaning of the French word **jour** is day?

Jour is embedded within the word '**jour**ney' – a day's travel. It is also the jour in the word '**jour**nal' – such as the one you're holding in your hands right now!

Flip back through this journal and you'll see your journey so far; the tools, the practices, the scribbles, the doodles and the days you've dedicated to growing your unique gorgeousness. From now on, with each day that passes, each experience you have, each person you meet and every landscape of life you move into, you'll navigate your way through with a powerful set of tools in your backpack. Yes, there'll be hiccups. There'll be mishaps. There'll be mistakes and retakes and apparent wrong turns – as well as many right ones! Yet, each bend in the pathway will allow you to grow further, delve deeper and become another step closer to who you were born to be.

My hope is that you will put this journal somewhere safe; maybe in a drawer or a box of treasured things and that you will keep it until you are much older. Perhaps one day you will look back at *REBEL BEAUTY FOR TEENS* and realise that it was a valuable part of becoming the greatest version of you. Maybe you'll reread it and discover the original seeds of dreams that have long since grown into mighty trees that shape your life. Or perhaps you'll find a window to your past self... and realise just how far you have come.

Or maybe you'll forget the book... but everything you've learnt in its pages will power you forwards anyway. Whatever happens, I wish you many beautiful days.

Bethan